A Life of Christ
for Children

A Life of Christ for Children

As Told by a Grandmother

Adapted from the French of
Mme. La Comtesse de Ségur

by

Mary Virginia Merrick

ANGELUS PRESS
2915 FOREST AVENUE
KANSAS CITY, MISSOURI 64109

Nihil Obstat
F.G. Holweck
Censor Librorum

Imprimatur
Joannes J. Glennon
Archbishop of St. Louis

September 25, 1909

Originally published by B. Herder Book Co. Second edition, 1919.

ANGELUS PRESS

2915 FOREST AVENUE
KANSAS CITY, MISSOURI 64109
PHONE (816) 753-3150
FAX (816) 753-3557
ORDER LINE 1-800-966-7337
www.angeluspress.org

ISBN 978-1-892331-80-9
FIRST PRINTING–July 2010

Printed in the United States of America

FOREWORD.

Our Holy Father, Pius X., at the beginning of his pontificate, issued a great letter to the whole world, in which he said that it was the desire of his heart to restore all things in Christ. Small as our share must be in such a great work, we can, at least, as faithful children of our Holy Father, begin with ourselves and strive to make our own life an imitation of the Life of Jesus of Nazareth. To know Him in the flesh, how He lived and talked and acted when He was upon earth, should surely be to us not only of the greatest interest, but also the most inspiring call to action and faithful service. Our dear Lord was simplicity itself, and the translator of the present work has put before us in simple language that story—the greatest that the world has ever known. To make ourselves familiar with the life of Jesus Christ from Bethlehem to Calvary, and to the Mount of the Ascension, is a most efficacious way to warm our souls with a love for Him who died that we might live, a most sure way of having Him with us through all the days of our life, and even in the hour when He calls us unto that land where He waits for us.

J. CARD. GIBBONS.

PREFACE

This volume presents to its young readers in a manner suited to their age the life on earth of our Blessed Lord. We follow Him in this story related for us by His own immediate followers in the pages of the Holy Gospel.

We see him as an infant, a child, a grown boy, and then, in the fullness of His power, as a man.

His whole life is worthy of our study because nothing begins to compare in value, either in time or eternity, with the life of Jesus Christ.

Nothing is more beneficial to the young boy or girl of to-day than a knowledge of that Life. He will find in it the instruction that he most needs; he will find therein how to live as a boy and afterwards as a man; and, in imitating Christ, he will bring out the very best that is in himself, both from an earthly and a heavenly stand-point.

We must remember that Jesus Christ came down from heaven and became a man and lived His human life to show us how we ought to live. There is no one to whom He does not speak directly through that life, and it is just as valuable, just as practical, now as it was in the days when Christ walked upon earth. As we grow up and meet the little or big things of everyday life, we are called upon to show our worth and our character, or to show that we haven't anything of either—which God forbid.

Every day we are called upon to do this little work of study or of errands at home; to keep our temper in this game or under this trial; to be pure, not to seek to satisfy our curiosity, or our senses, by indulging in this pleasure or in that; to keep to our religious duties; to love our parents, our brothers, our sisters, with a real, unselfish love. We are called upon to stand for honesty; for fair play; for truthfulness; for purity and cleanliness of life—all through our days.

All these calls must come to every one of us; they do come every day. And it is equally true that we need the example, the lesson of One Who actually faced all the evils of the world: Who had pain and suffering and yet Who conquered all and won out in all. Jesus Christ was a man among men, and in His manhood He gave an example of what every man should be; of what every one of us should be. In every case that comes before us where we must ask ourselves whether we will do this or that, whether we will refrain from this forbidden pleasure or yield to it, in every case we can readily see—since we know Him—what Jesus Christ would have done and what He would wish us to do. There is no uncertainty about it; there is no doubt about it. Before us, as a great light, the greatest light the world has ever known; greater and more piercing than the sun, illuminating every soul, is the life of Jesus Christ. He has given His example, He has shown what ought to be done in every case to every boy and girl, every man and woman.

To show forth the splendor and the practical value of that Life has been the object of this Grandmother's Story. It has been a work of much labor, but of greater love. We wish that our children would study it; read it over time and time again; read the Gospels from which it is taken; sit down quietly now and again and think of our Lord Jesus, think of how we ourselves are imitating Him; and always, day and night, pray to Him in utter confidence and childlike affection and frankness and love. Then, indeed, will you love Him even more than you do, and the sweetest, most gracious comfort in your life will be the personal love that you bear to Jesus Christ; and nothing, no sin of any kind, will ever separate you from Him. That love will be your abiding support, and upon it you will find that you can lean when all else fails.

May the knowledge and the love of Him sink deep into your hearts; so deep that nothing will ever be strong enough or alluring enough to root it out. Live for Him; grow like unto Him; and then, as He was, so will you be, kind and patient and pure and hopeful. In the Sacrament of the Holy Eucharist will you possess Him as your very own; then will you speak to Him and He to you, and the glories that your soul will know in its communions with Him through life will be unfolded, in all their fullness when he asks you to come to Him in the Kingdom where He now reigns.

JOHN J. BURKE, C. S. P.

INTRODUCTION

Sophie, Comtesse de Segur, was born in the year 1799 in Russia. Her father was the Count Rostopschine who at that time was Prime Minister to the Emperor Paul. The Czar stood Godfather to little Sophie who was baptized in the Greek Church, which later on in life Sophie renounced to embrace the Catholic faith.

Sophie's childhood and girlhood were spent in Russia as one of a large and happy family of brothers and sisters.

At an early age she met and married the Count de Segur of France, in which country she ever afterwards resided.

This happy union was blessed with many children, one of whom became Monseigneur de Segur, so well beloved in Paris, where for many years he exercised his priestly ministry. His numerous writings, numbering at least one hundred brochures, or small books, testify to his piety and love of little children.

This affection for the lambs of his flock, Monseigneur de Segur imbibed from his mother, all her life a lover of children. When time had lessened her maternal cares Mme. de Segur found her greatest happiness in living over, in the company of her grandchildren, the years of her motherhood. She was the devoted grandmother of thirteen little ones, whose greatest delight was to listen to the stories she could so well tell and to which their mothers had listened as eagerly.

It was not until late in life that Mme de Segur committed to writing these charming tales, and which to this day are read with delight by the children over the sea.

Among these tales none was listened to with greatest interest than that wonderful story of God become man, and for thirty-three years making our earth his home.

We can picture this happy band of little ones gathered on a bright morning in grandma's sunny room and begging for the promised story of Christ.

There they all are, Camille and her sister Madeleine, Elizabeth and her four brothers, Pierre, Henry, Louis, and Jack, and their cousins, Henrietta and Jane, Valentine, Mary, Theresa, and even Paul and little Louis, only five years old, all eager to hear.

The sunlight streams in on expectant faces, on golden curles, brown hair, and grandma's white head. The canary sings his loudest while the children scramble for the places at grandma's right and left.

Finally all are seated, and grandma, seated in her big armchair, begins THE STORY OF CHRIST.

INDEX.

BOOK FIRST

The Childhood of Jesus.

BOOK SECOND

First Year of the Ministry of Jesus.

BOOK THIRD.

Second Year of the Ministry of Jesus.

BOOK FOURTH.

Third Year of the Ministry of Jesus.

BOOK FIFTH.

The Last Days in the Ministry of Jesus.

BOOK SIXTH.

The Passion and the Resurrection of Jesus.

BOOK FIRST

The Childhood of Jesus

CHAPTER I.

THE JEWS.

Grandma: I am about to tell you the story of Jesus Christ, the Son of God, the Second Person of the Blessed Trinity; God made man to redeem us from sin and eternal death. I may in the course of this wonderful story use words which the little ones may not understand, do not fail to interrupt me and ask any question you wish.

The Jews were a people favored by God. Over this nation he watched with special care. To them he had foretold through his servants, the prophets, the coming of his Son, Jesus Christ, who was to be born among them and who was to save them from the evil ones.

The Jews should have been very good, being so blessed by God, but they were often wicked and rebelled against God and against the kings God appointed over them; but God is so good and merciful that he forgives as often as we repent and beg his forgiveness, and as often as the Jews fell into sin and repented, God would forgive them, but unfortunately they would fall again.

God had given them a beautiful country which was called Judea and later on was called Palestine.

There they lived and waited for this Savior, whose coming the prophets had foretold centuries before.

They thought the Son of God would come in great glory, as the most powerful and the richest of kings; that he would have a large following and immense wealth.

While they were waiting and studying the words of the prophets, and disputing among themselves concerning this promised Messias and the time of his coming, Jesus Christ, the Son of God, our Lord and Savior, was about to be born in Judea.

CHAPTER II.

THE ANNUNCIATION.

Joachim and Anna, two faithful servants of God who were descended from the great Jewish king, David, were blessed with a daughter named Mary.

At the age of fifteen Mary was espoused to her cousin, Joseph, who was also of the House of David.

Mary was the most beautiful, the wisest, and the most perfect of all God's creatures. One day while she was praying in her home at Nazareth, suddenly before her stood a beautiful angel, resplendent with light. It was the Angel Gabriel, God's messenger, and he said to Mary: "Hail, full of grace, the Lord is with thee; blessed art thou among women." At these words of the angel Mary grew troubled, because she was very humble and never thought of her many virtues, and considered herself therefore unworthy of being spoken to by the angel as "blessed among women."

While thinking within herself what such a greeting might mean, the angel spoke again and said to her: "Fear not, Mary, thou hast found grace with God. Thou shalt bring forth a son, and thou shalt call his name Jesus. He shall be great, and shall be called the Son of the Most High; and the Lord God shall give unto him the throne of David, his father; and he shall reign forever, and of his kingdom there shall be no end."

And Mary said to the angel: "How shall this be done?" The Angel answering said to her:

"The Holy Ghost shall come upon thee, and the power of the Most High shall overshadow thee. And therefore also the Holy which shall be born of thee shall be called the Son of God."

The angel added that in three months her cousin, Elizabeth, who was old, and whom people mocked and called sterile, would also have a son, to show that nothing was impossible to God.

And Mary said: "Behold the handmaid of the Lord; be it done to me according to thy word." And the angel left her—

Elizabeth: Grandma, why did the angel say that people mocked Elizabeth because she was sterile? What is sterile?

Grandma: Sterile means that she had never had a child. The Jews considered this a great disgrace, because every Jew hoped that Jesus, the Messias, promised by God to deliver the world from sin, would be born in their family, and when a Jew was not blessed with children he could not cherish this hope.

Henry: And why did the angel say he would be great? How would he be great?

Grandma: The angel meant he would be great in holiness and in power.

Louis: Why did the angel say he would reign forever? He did not reign at all, and doesn't reign now.

Grandma: The angel spoke of the spiritual kingdom of Jesus over the whole world. The kingdom of Jesus is the Church. The pope, the bishops, and the priests of the Church have been working for eighteen hundred years to establish the kingdom of Jesus Christ on this earth. Our Lord has returned to Heaven where he now is, where he will be forever, and whence he reigns and rules over all men; where he rewards the good and punishes the wicked.

Now, I shall tell you the story of the Visitation, that is to say, the visit of the Blessed Virgin Mary to her cousin, Elizabeth, the wife of Zachary, a priest of the temple of Jerusalem.

Jane: What is a temple?

Grandma: The temple was for the Jews what the church is for us. It was the house of God. In the temple they kept the commandments of God written on tables of stone, which they called the "Tables of the Law."

It was here all sacred things were preserved, and it was in the temple the Jews gathered together to offer up their sacrifices.

CHAPTER III.

THE VISITATION.

Zachary was a Jewish priest. He and his wife, Elizabeth, were very old. Elizabeth was eighty years of age. They had no children, which saddened them greatly.

Henry: Did the Jewish priests marry?

Grandma: Yes, the priests of the Jewish law married, because the old law was not as perfect as our law, and did not exact of the priests a life of such absolute devotion and renunciation.

Our priests have no wives, in order that they may devote themselves more exclusively to the service of God, to the salvation of souls, to the relief of the poor, and to the religious instruction of children.

One day Zachary entered the temple to offer incense to God at the alter of the sanctuary.

The people remained outside, praying. According to the Jewish custom, the priests alone had the right to enter this part of the temple. While Zachary was praying and burning incense, he saw an angel standing at the right of the alter.

Zachary was troubled and frightened at the apparition of an angel, but the angel said to him:

"Fear not, Zachary, for thy prayer is heard; and thy wife, Elizabeth, shall bear a son, and thou shalt call his name John. And thou shalt have joy and gladness, and many shall rejoice in his nativity. He shall be filled with the Holy Ghost, and he shall convert many of the children of Isreal to the Lord their God."

Zachary found it difficult to believe the words of the angel, and said to him:

"Whereby shall I know this? for I am an old man, and my wife is advanced in years."

The Angel answered:

"I am Gabriel, who stand before God; and am sent to speak to thee, and to bring thee these good tidings. And behold, thou shalt be dumb, and shalt not be able to speak until the day wherein these things shall come to pass, because thou hast not believed my words, which shall be fulfilled in their time."

And the angel disappeared.

When Zachary came out of the temple the people asked him why he had tarried so long inside; but he could not answer, for he was dumb.

A short while after this Zachary knew the angel's promise would soon be fulfilled and that Elizabeth would have a son.

Elizabeth rejoiced and thanked God who had now taken from her the humilation under which she had so long lived.

While Elizabeth was praising God for this great favor, her cousin, the Virgin Mary, who knew of this good news from the angel, asked her spouse, Joseph, to take her to visit Elizabeth. Joseph consented, and they set out on foot for the city of Hebron, where dwelt Elizabeth, across the hills of Judea.

When Mary entered the house she greeted her cousin, Elizabeth. As soon as Elizabeth heard Mary's voice she was filled with the Holy Ghost, who revealed to her that Mary was to be the mother of the Son of God, and she cried out:

"Blessed art thou among women, and blessed is the fruit of thy womb. And whence is this (honor) to me, that the mother of my Lord should come to me?" To whom Mary replied in the words of that beautiful hymn of thanksgiving, called the "Magnificat," which is sung in Church at the end of Vespers.

After Mary had spent three months with her cousin, Elizabeth, she returned to her own home in Nazareth.

CHAPTER IV.

BIRTH OF JOHN THE BAPTIST.

At the time predicted by the Angel Gabriel Elizabeth gave birth to a son. On hearing this glad news many came to congratulate her, for Elizabeth had long desired a son, and had prayed fervently that she might one day be a mother. On the eighth day after the birth of the child, according to the custom of the Jewish people, the priests came to circumcise him.

Henry: What does circumcise mean?

Grandma: Circumcision was the mark of the Jewish religion, and when administered the child received its name as do Christians when they receive baptism.

The priests, therefore, wished to circumcise the child, and to give him his father's name, Zachary. But Elizabeth said to them: "Not so; he shall be called John." But they replied: "There is none of thy kindred called by that name." In Hebrew John signified full of grace.

As Elizabeth insisted, Zachary was asked to indicate in some way what should be the child's name.

Zachary, taking a writing tablet, wrote: "John is his name."

This surprised every one, and, at that moment Zachary's tongue was loosed miraculously, and he began to speak and to praise God.

All those present and all the people of the neighborhood were filled with wonder and admiration. And they came from far and wide to see this child, whose birth was accompanied by such miracles; and they said to one another: "What a one, think ye, this child shall be? For the hand of the Lord was with him."

And John grew and increased in strength and was remarkably intelligent, and when he grew older he withdrew into the desert.

Mary: What is a desert?

Grandma: The desert is a desolate place of sandy soil in which nothing can grow. John withdrew into the desert to prepare for his great mission of Precursor; that is to say, forerunner of Christ. He was to announce the coming of Jesus, the Savior of the world. .   .   .

CHAPTER V.

THE BIRTH OF JESUS CHRIST. ADORATION OF THE SHEPHERDS.

Grandma: Shortly before the birth of Jesus, Augustus Caesar, Emperor of Rome and ruler of Judea, ordered that a census be taken of all the inhabitants of the countries under his rule. Cyrinus, Governor of Syria, obeying this injunction, issued an edict that all the people of Syria and Judea should be enrolled, each in the city of his forefathers. At this time Joseph lived in Nazareth, a city of Galilee, and to be enrolled according to this command of Ceasar's he was obliged to travel to Bethlehem, a little town in the province of Judea, near Jerusalem, about twenty-five miles from Nazareth. Bethlehem was the city of David and of his family, and you remember that I told you that Joseph and Mary were of the family of David. He set out, therefore, with Mary his espoused wife.

The journey was long and Mary was very weary when they reached Bethlehem, and Joseph anxiously sought a shelter for his spouse, but everywhere he was refused. A large concourse of people had come to this city to be enrolled, "and there was no room for them in the inn."

When Joseph was turned away from the inn, not knowing where to turn to find a resting place for Mary, he wandered outside of the city, and there, near the gates of the city, he found a cave, which served as a stable to shelter cows and mules.

Tradition tells us that King David had often rested in this cave when, as a shepherd, he watched his flocks nearby. There Joseph prepared for Mary a bed of straw, and in that stable of Bethlehem Jesus came into the world. In the country round about Bethlehem, as in the days of King David, there were shepherds keeping watch over their flocks by day and night for fear they might be stolen or harm come to them. Suddenly, in the middle of the night "an angel of the Lord stood by them, and the brightness of God shone round about them; and they feared with a great fear; but the angel said to them: Fear not; for, behold, I bring you good tidings of great joy, that shall be to all the people; for this day is born to you a Savior, who is Christ the Lord, in the city of David. And this shall be a sign unto you. You shall find the Infant wrapped in swaddling clothes, and laid in a manger."

Jane: What is a manger?

Grandma: A manger is a kind of trough out of which the animals of the stable eat.

John: But the poor infant must have been very uncomfortable in such a cradle.

Grandma: Yes; he was poorly cradled and clothed, but God so willed it.

Jane: How was it that God, who is his father, and who made all things, did not give him a nice cradle and a beautiful home, instead of letting him lie in a manger in a miserable stable?

Grandma: Because the Child Jesus wished to show us, by his example, that we must not desire the riches of this world, nor set our hearts on those things that wealth can give; and that we must love privations and humiliations.

Louise: I don't want to lie in a manger nor live in a stable.

Grandma: We are not obliged to sleep in a stable, but we *are* called upon not to be too exacting or too fond of our own ease and comfort.

After the angel had told the shepherds how they were to recognize the Child, "there was suddenly with the angel a multitude of the heavenly army, praising God, and saying: 'Glory to God in the highest; and on earth peace to men of good will.'" After the angels left the shepherds "they said to one another, let us go over to Bethlehem, and let us see this Word that has come to pass, which the Lord hath showed to us. And they came with haste; and found Mary and Joseph, and the infant lying in a manger." And when they saw the Child they adored him and they understood the words of the angel.

All those to whom the shepherds told of this first Christmas night wondered at the marvelous things they heard. And Mary, the mother of Jesus, kept in her heart the memory of all these things and dwelt on them lovingly.

At the end of eight days the Child was circumcised, and the name of Jesus was given him, as the Angel Gabriel had told Mary before his coming.

CHAPTER VI.

THE WISE MEN.

Shortly after these events news came to Herod that there were strangers in Jerusalem, Wise Men from the East, and that they were asking of every one: "Where is he that is born King of the Jews? For we have seen his star in the east, and are come to adore him."

When Herod heard this, he was alarmed, for he feared that a king greater than he should come and take from him his kingdom.

He sent, therefore, for the Wise Men and questioned them and learnt that the king of whom they spoke and whom they sought was Christ, the Messias, whose coming the Jews expected as foretold to them by the prophets.

Then Herod sent for the priests, the scribes, and all the learned men of Jerusalem and inquired of them where the Christ was to be born. And they answered: "In Bethlehem of Judea. For so it is written by the prophet."

And calling aside the Wise Men he questioned them with great care as to the time the star had appeared to them.

The Wise Men, who are also called the Magi, told Herod that the coming of Jesus Christ had been revealed to them, and that a star, larger and more beautiful than all the other stars of the heavens, had appeared in the east as a sign to them of the birth of this promised Messias, Jesus Christ, the Son of God. They related how they had immediately set out to find him, the star going before them and guiding them on their way. They added that this star had disappeared as they reached Jerusalem, and there fore they were eagerly asking to see this King of the Jews, whose coming had been foretold to them, and whom they had come so far to seek that they might adore him.

Herod thanked them and told them to go to Bethlehem, for it had been foretold that in that city would be born the Messias who was to save all men and deliver them from the power of the evil one.

"Go," he said, "and diligently inquire after the Child, and when you have found him, bring me word again, that I also may come and adore him."

The Magi set out again, and immediately the star reappeared, and "seeing the star they rejoiced with exceeding great joy," and it went before them, as it had done in their long journeyings "until it came and stood over the cave where the Child was."

The Magi, with joy in their hearts, entered the stable, "and there they found the Child with Mary his mother, and falling down they adored him; and opening their treasures, they offered him gifts: gold, frankincense, and myrrh."

Jack: Is incense a treasure? I don't think that is much of a gift. We burn it in all our churches.

Grandma: The incense we burn is a resin, a kind of gum, which flows from certain trees; but it has not the delicious fragrance of the incense of Arabia and Judea. This incense was, and still is, very rare and costly.

Jack: But what could the Child Jesus and his mother do with it? It seems a very useless gift to me.

Grandma: The Magi offered incense, not only as a precious and valuable gift, but as an homage, as an act of worship, showing by this offering that they recognized this Child as the Son of God, for incense is offered only to God.

Henrietta: What is myrrh?

Grandma: Myrrh is a very precious perfume; very bitter to the taste. This gift signified that Jesus was to suffer much to atone for the sins of men, and would finally die to save mankind. All this God had revealed to the Magi.

After having adored the Child, the Wise Men made ready to return to their own country. But before setting out, an angel appeared to them in their sleep and commanded them to go back another way, forbidding them to return to Herod in Jerusalem, and warning them that Herod only wished to find the Child that he might put him to death.

In the meanwhile Herod waited and grew impatient at their delay, and wondered that they failed to return to him as he had commanded them to do.

CHAPTER VII.

THE PRESENTATION IN THE TEMPLE.
THE FLIGHT INTO EGYPT.

After the return of the Magi to their own country it was time when, according to the law of Moses, Mary was obliged to go to Jerusalem to present the Child Jesus in the Temple and offer a sacrifice.

Joseph and Mary offered two turtle doves, as the customary offering of the poor. The rich always offered a lamb.

Louis: Why were doves and lambs offered? To whom were they offered?

Grandma: According to the law of the Jews as, all men belonged to God, parents were obliged to offer their children to God as soon as possible after their birth for the service of the Temple.

After making this offering, however, they were allowed to take back their infants, leaving in their stead offerings of turtle doves or lambs, according to their means. The high priests received these offerings and killed them and offered them to the Lord as a sacrifice agreeable to him.

Paul: But this was not true, was it, grandma?

Grandma: Oh, yes; it was true. God was pleased with these sacrifices because they were offered in obedience to the law, and God delights in obedience.

Elizabeth: But why had God commanded sacrifices? How could the blood of animals be agreeable to him?

Grandma: The blood of these animals was not in itself agreeable to God, but only because it prefigured the sacrifice of the cross, by which divine sacrifice Jesus Christ was to save us. The day the Virgin Mary and her husband, Joseph, carried the Infant Jesus to the Temple, they found there an old man named Simeon who was a just man and obedient to the law of God. It had been revealed to him that before his eyes closed in death he would see the Messias, Christ, the Son of God.

When, therefore, the Child was brought into the Temple the Spirit of God made known to Simeon that this Child was the Messias he expected; the promised Redeemer, who was to save all men.

Simeon took the Child Jesus in his arms, and with great joy began to glorify God, saying:

"Now thou dost dismiss thy servant in peace, O Lord, according to thy word, because my eyes have seen thy salvation which thou hast prepared before the face of all thy people."

While Simeon continued thus praising God, and saying sublime things of the Child and of his mother, an old woman named Anna, who was a prophetess, a widow of eighty-four years of age, entered the

Temple, and she too began to praise the Lord and to speak of the Child Jesus as the one whose coming the Jews had long looked for to deliver them from the power of the evil one.

Louis: And how did Simeon know that Jesus was the Messias?

Grandma: It was told to him by the Holy Ghost speaking within him without words.

Jack: How could Simeon understand when the Holy Ghost spoke without words?

Grandma: It is possible for the Holy Ghost, the Spirit of God, who is God equal to the Father and the Son, to make himself understood to a soul without use of words, as it is possible to you, for instance, to think of your father and mother when absent from them, and to recall the words they have spoken to you. However, for us, to whom God has not granted such favors, it is not easy to understand what passes between God and the souls of his saints.

After the Presentation in the Temple Mary and Joseph returned to Bethlehem with the Child Jesus.

One night, as Joseph was sleeping, an angel appeared to him and said: "Arise, take the Child and his mother, and fly into Egypt; and be there until I shall tell thee. For it will come to pass that Herod will seek the Child to destroy him." And Joseph rose at once and woke Mary and told her the message of the angel, and they made ready and set out immediately for Egypt.

Jack: How did they travel without a carriage?

Grandma: Tradition tells us they journeyed with an ass. Joseph seated Mary on the donkey with the Child Jesus in her arms, and he walked beside them leading the donkey. Thus they fled to Egypt in the darkness of the night, so that no human eye could see them or human tongue tell Herod which way they had gone.

Jack: But why, grandma, as the Child Jesus was the Son of God, did he not order that Herod be put to death?

Grandma: Because Jesus did not come on earth to destroy the wicked, but to convert them, and, moreover, he wished to suffer all these trails for love of us, to teach us to bear patiently our burdens in this life.

CHAPTER VIII.

THE MASSACRE OF THE INNOCENTS.

Herod still waited for the return of the Wise Men, and finally, when he gave up hope of seeing them again, he grew very angry, for he realized that, without their aid, he could not find the Child-king, whose birth the Magi had announced to him, and whose coming he greatly feared would deprive him of his kingdom. He had determined to put this Child to death, but how could he accomplish this evil deed, not knowing where he dwelt?

Therefore, he resolved to kill all children aged two years and under, feeling sure that the Child Jesus would be among the children of that age. So this cruel king ordered his soldiers, who were as wicked as he, to go to Bethlehem sword in hand and massacre all children of tender years.

Louis: What a horrible man! How terrible! The poor parents must have cried as much as their little ones.

Grandma: They certainly did, and I must tell you that a long time before this event happened a prophet named Jeremias—

Louis: And what is a prophet?

Grandma: A prophet is a man to whom God gives the gift of being able to know and tell beforehand things that will happen.

Louis: What—he can tell what has not yet happened?

Henrietta: It is as if the good Lord gave me this gift and I should know beforehand and say to you: To-night you will be naughty and to-morrow you will be punished, and in ten years you will die; and then, if it all happened, I would be a prophet. Is that not so, grandma?

Grandma (smiling): No; in that case you would be a prophetess. Fortunately you are not one, as your prophecies would not be very agreeable to Louis; but I see you understand what a prophet is, and you have explained it very well. The prophets, however, predicted only what concerned the glory of God and the good of mankind. I was about to tell you that a prophet, named Jeremias, had predicted this calamity, this horrible crime, which is called: "The Massacre of the Innocents." He had foretold that in that day there would be "lamentations and great mourning."

You can picture this sad scene: little children torn from the protecting arms of their mothers, who were running hither and thither striving in vain to save their precious babies from the cruel soldiers, who put them to death by the sword. Thus perished in one day many children in Bethlehem and the surrounding country. These little innocents were the first martyrs, the first to give their life for Christ, and we celebrate their feast after Christmas, on December the twenty-eighth.

After Joseph and Mary and the Child Jesus had remained some time in Egypt, an angel appeared to Joseph in his sleep and said to him: "Arise and take the Child and his mother and go into the land of Israel, for they are dead that sought the life of the Child."

Jack: Did Herod repent before he died?

Grandma: No; he died, as he had lived, a wicked king.

Joseph, who never hesitated for a moment to obey the commands of God, took the Child and his mother and set out at once for Judea. On the journey he learnt that Archelaus, son of Herod, had been made king at his father's death; and being afraid, Joseph retired into the province of Galilee, to a city called Nazareth. That Jesus should live in Nazareth had also been predicted by the prophets.

And now, children, I shall tell you how the Child Jesus was lost in Jerusalem.

Paul: Why, who lost the Child Jesus?

Grandma: I shall tell you of this the next time we meet.

CHAPTER IX.

JESUS AMONG THE DOCTORS.

The Child Jesus lived in Nazareth with his mother and his foster-father, St. Joseph. As he grew older he worked with his father, who earned his livelihood as a carpenter, for the Holy Family was poor. All who knew the Child Jesus admired his wisdom, goodness, and gentleness.

Every year at the Feast of the Pasch—

John: What was the Feast of the Pasch?

Grandma: The Feast of the Pasch, or Passover, was the celebration by the Jewish people of their passage over the Red Sea, when the Lord had delivered them from the Egyptian bondage.

Louis: How was the feast celebrated?

Grandma: Each family killed a kid or a lamb, which was roasted whole and eaten with great ceremony at a family feast, to which all the relatives were invited. They ate standing and in traveling garb, staff in hand, to remind them of their long journeyings when God had led them from their captivity in Egypt to the promised land.

The feast of the Passover lasted seven days. Every year Mary and Joseph went to Jerusalem to celebrate this feast. When the Child Jesus had reached his twelfth year he accompanied his parents, as prescribed by the Jewish law. This initation of a child to the ceremonies of the Passover was regarded as an event in the family life. When the feast was over the visitors who had gathered in Jerusalem departed in family groups or caravans, each to his own home. Mary and Joseph set out with their friends and relations and did not perceive that Jesus was not with them, or perhaps they thought him in the company of his young companions, and his absence passed unnoticed till the band stopped at eventide for refreshment and rest.

Not finding the Child Jesus in their company they searched anxiously for him among the crowd of wayfarers, and retracing their steps to Jerusalem inquired eagerly of all the travelers they met. For three days and nights, neither eating nor drinking, Mary and Joseph continued their search, sorrowfully; but the Child Jesus was not to be found.

Finally they entered the Temple and there they found the Child, "sitting in the midst of the doctors, hearing them and asking them questions," and explaining to them obscure passages of the sacred writings so clearly that the Doctors of the Law "and all that heard him were astonished at his wisdom and his answers."

Mary and Joseph were much surprised at what they saw and heard, and his mother, approaching her Son, said to him: "Son, why hast thou done so to us? behold thy father and I have sought thee sorrowing." Jesus answered gravely: "How is it that you sought me? did you not know that I must be about my Father's business?" "And they understood not the words that he spoke to them." They did not know that the business which already occupied this Divine Child was to make men believe and understand that he, Jesus, was the Son of God, the Christ, the Messias expected by the Jewish nation. None the less Jesus, rising, followed his parents, for if in divine matters he obeyed his heavenly Father, in all else he obeyed implicity his mother, Mary, and St. Joseph.

They returned to Nazareth, where they lived and where St. Joseph died, and the Child Jesus grew "and advanced in wisdom and age and grace with God and man." "And his mother kept all these words in her heart." She kept in her memory all the words and actions of Jesus.

From his twelfth to his thirtieth year our Lord did naught but obey, work, and pray; thus becoming a living example for all Christians, and most especially for all children and young people.

What child is there who will dare refuse to obey and to work, when the Son of God himself has left us such an example?

St. Joseph died peacefully in the arms of Jesus and
Mary, and for this reason he has always been regarded as the patron of the dying.

BOOK SECOND

First Year of the Ministry of Jesus

CHAPTER X.

ST. JOHN THE BAPTIST. BAPTISM OF CHRIST.

Grandma: No doubt, my children, you remember that John the Baptist lived in the desert preparing for his mission of Precursor of Christ. He increased in sanctity as he grew older. He prayed unceasingly, and led a very penitential life, his food being of locusts and wild honey and his garments of camel's hair. At about thirty years of age he came out of the desert and began to preach. He spoke eloquently of God, of the reward of heaven, and the punishment of hell, and of the necessity of doing penance, and everywhere, in all the country round about the Jordan, he announced to all men the coming of the Savior.

Many flocked to hear John, and he taught them to repent of their sins, and he baptized in the Jordan all who confessed their sins and asked for baptism.

Louis: What is the Jordan; and how did John baptize.

Grandma: The Jordan is a river which flows a few miles from Jerusalem. Those who wished to be baptized went down into the Jordan a few feet from the shore and John baptized them by pouring on their heads water from this stream. This he did to show the purity of heart which should be theirs.

The people surrounded John the Baptist and asked of him guidance and advice. To the rich he said: He that hath two coats, let him give to him that hath none; and he that hath meat, let him do in like manner." And to the Publicans who came to ask what they should do, he said; "Do nothing more than that which is appointed you."

Henrietta: Who are the "Publicans;" and what was appointed them to do?

Grandma: The Publicans were men employed by the Romans—who, as you know, were the rulers of Judea and of the Jews—to collect the taxes; that is, the money every one was obliged to pay for the support of the roads, bridges, and highways. Moreover, a portion of this money was sent to Rome for the use of the Emperor.

Often these Publicans demanded of the people more than was due, and consequently the Jews hated them and called them thieves, and John was reproving them for imposing on the people these unjust taxes.

To the soldiers, who also asked his good counsel, he said. "Do violence to no man, neither calumniate any man, and be content with your pay."

The people who heard John found in him so much virtue, goodness, and wisdom that they took him to be the Christ, the promised Messias, whose coming was expected at this time as announced by the prophets; but John said: "There cometh after me one mightier than I, the latchet of whose shoe I am not worthy to stoop down and loose. I have baptized you with water, but he shall baptize you with the Holy Ghost."

King Herod, the son of the former Herod, who had succeeded his brother Archelaus, wished to know John and to hear him speak; but instead of flattering the vanity of the king, and praising him, John reproved him for the wicked life he was leading. This angered Herod, but he dared not harm John, for he feared him by reason of his sanctity and also because of the great esteem in which the people held him.

About this time, after the death of Joseph, Jesus left Nazareth, and sought John on the banks of the Jordan to be baptized by him. John, who knew that Jesus was the Son of God, the Second Person of the Blessed Trinity, refused, out of reverence, to baptize him: "I ought to be baptized by thee, and comest thou to me?" John said; and Jesus answered: "Suffer it to be so now, for so it becometh us to fulfill all justice."

Then John refused no longer, and pouring water on the head of Jesus he baptized him.

As Jesus came out of the water, suddenly the heavens were opened and the Holy Ghost descended in the form of a dove and rested on his head, and a voice from heaven said: "This is my beloved Son in whom I am well pleased."

Henrietta: Whose voice was this?

Grandma: This was the voice of God the Father, who thus announced to the world that Jesus Christ was truly his only Son, both God and man.

Jack: How old was our Lord when he was baptized?

Grandma: About thirty years of age. He had left Nazareth and was about to start on his journeyings through Judea, in order to show himself to the world and to instruct men in the true law which leads to salvation.

CHAPTER XI.

JESUS IN THE DESERT. THE TEMPTATION.

Before instructing the Jews and revealing to them that he was truly the incarnate Son of God, our Lord wished to give us an example of mortification and penance.

Louise: What does that mean—mortification?

Grandma: To mortify means to deny ourselves, to punish ourselves.

Louise: And why should we punish our bodies? What wrong has my body done? It seems to me it only obeys my wishes.

Grandma: You are mistaken. Your body has evil inclinations which lead you to desire things forbidden by God; such as laziness, gluttony, anger, and other evil tendencies. It is just, therefore, to do penance; to deny and to punish the body which so frequently leads us into sin.

Henrietta: And supposed I don't do penance.

Grandma: If we don't do penance, the good Lord will punish us after death, and more severely than we ourselves would have done. Therefore, it is wiser to mortify ourselves while we live that we may not remain long in Purgatory, where we expiate the sins for which we have not atoned in this world. On the other hand, if at our death our Lord finds in us no sins unpunished, none for which we have not atoned, he bids us at once to enter into the joys of heaven, with the Blessed Virgin, the angels, and saints, and to rejoice with them forever.

As I was saying, Jesus wished to give us an example of mortification; for this purpose he withdrew into the desert.

Louis: Was it the same desert where John lived?

Grandma: Yes; the same, but not the same part, and, moreover, John had left the desert about a year previously.

Mary: Where was John when Jesus went into the desert?

Grandma: He was journeying from place to place through Judea and Galilee, proclaiming the advent of the Messias, in order that Jesus might find the people prepared to recognize and adore the Savior. Jesus went into the desert alone, and remained there fasting for forty days.

Henrietta: Why, Grandma, that is impossible; he would have died of hunger!

Grandma: If our Lord had been a man such as we are, he would certainly have died, and in less time than forty days; but do not forget that Jesus was God made man, and that he could and willed to suffer to an extraordinary degree from hunger and from thirst to expiate our sins of gluttony, sloth, indolence, and sensuality.

Jane: What is sensuality?

Grandma: It is the love of all that is agreeable to the body; to love to eat well, to drink well, to be always comfortable; in a word, to love our own ease and to be unwilling to bear any discomfort.

Henrietta: But I see no harm in all that.

Grandma: At first sight this does not seem wrong, but in fact, when we live thus, we become indolent, incapable of making any sacrifice for the sake of duty. We think only of pleasures, of fun, and of spending our time in amusements. We forget heaven, we forget we are sinners and have sins to expiate. In fact, we risk losing our souls, as you will see by the story of the bad rich man.

While Jesus was in the desert, the devil, who was surprised and angry that he had never been able to make Jesus commit the smallest sin, determined to take advantage of the hunger and weakness of Jesus after his long fast and, by tempting him, lead him into some fault. He approached Jesus and promised him food, saying: "If you are the Son of God, command that these stones be made bread."

Jesus answered Satan, saying: "It is written, not in bread alone doth man live, but in every word that proceedeth from the mouth of God."

The devil, seeing he was repulsed, and in doubt as to whether this Jesus was the promised Messias who was to deliver men from his evil power, tried another means to discover if Jesus was man or God. He took him to the city of Jerusalem and placed him on the pinnacle of the Temple. Then he said to him: "If thou be the Son of God, cast thyself down, for it is written: That he hath given his angels charge over thee, and in their hands shall they bear thee up, lest, perhaps, thou dash thy foot against a stone."

Jesus said to him: "It is written: Thou shalt not tempt the Lord thy God."

The devil, again overcome by the wisdom of the answers of Jesus, tried a third time to tempt him. He transported him to the top of a tall mountain, whence he showed him in an instant all the empires of the world and their glory, and said to him: "All these will I give thee if, falling down, thou wilt adore me."

Then Jesus said to him: "Begone, Satan, for it is written· The Lord thy God shalt thou adore, and him only shalt thou serve."

Then the devil, ashamed and baffled, withdrew and the angels approached Jesus and served him.

Paul: How glad I am that the devil left Jesus, but how did the angels serve him?

Grandma: They brought him food to eat, as far superior to what we eat in this world as Jesus himself was superior to all men and to the angels.

CHAPTER XII.

THE TESTIMONY OF JOHN. THE FIRST DISCIPLES
OF JESUS.

While Jesus was sustaining the struggle in the
desert, John the Baptist continued preaching
and baptizing along the banks of the Jordan.
Rumors reached Jerusalem that an extraordinary
man had appeared, and the question arose among
the Jews whether John might not be the Messias.
Priests and Levites were, therefore, sent to question
him.

Paul: Who were the Levites?

Grandma: The Levites assisted the priests in
the ceremonies of the Temple. They were below
the priests in rank, as a lieutenant is below a captain,
although both are officers. They came, therefore,
to John, questioning him if he were the Christ.
And he answered: "I am not the Christ;" and they
asked him: "What then? Art thou Elias?" And
he said: "I am not." "Art thou the prophet?"
And he answered: "No." They said therefore to
him: "Who art thou, that we may give an answer
to them that sent us? What sayest thou of thyself?"

John answered: "I am the voice of one crying in the wilderness; make straight the way of the Lord."

Thus John explained to them his mission of Precursor. They questioned him further as to why he baptized, since he was not the Christ, nor Elias, nor the prophet. John answered: "I baptize with water, but there hath stood one in the midst of you whom you know not; the latchet of whose shoe I am not worthy to loose. I saw the Spirit coming as a dove from heaven, and he remained upon him; he it is that baptizeth with the Holy Ghost. . . I saw and I gave testimony that this is the Son of God."

The following day John was walking with two of his disciples and Jesus passed by.

Louise: What are disciples?

Grandma: Disciples are scholars, friends, those who believe in the wisdom of a master and who follow him, and who endeavor to make others believe in his doctrine, that he may have many followers. When John saw Jesus he said: "Behold the Lamb of God." His two disciples hearing this left John and followed Jesus; and Jesus, turning and seeing them following him, said to them: "What seek you?" "Master, where dwellest thou?" they asked. Jesus replied: "Come and see," and they followed our Lord to his dwelling and remained with him all that day. One of these first two disciples was St. John, who became the beloved friend of Jesus, and who

wrote one of the four Gospels, or, as they are sometimes called Evangels, and he is therefore called
John the Evangelist. The other was St. Andrew.

After this long conversation with our Lord
Andrew met his brother Simon, a fisherman like
himself, and he said to him; "We have found the
Messias;" and he brought him to Jesus, and Jesus
looking upon him said: "Thou art Simon, the Son
of Jonas; thou shalt be called Peter." This was the
Apostle St. Peter, who was to be Head of the church.

The next day Jesus met Philip and he said to him:
"Follow me!" Philip was from Bethsaida, a city
in Galilee, and he followed Jesus with gladness,
for he had often heard of Christ from John the
Baptist.

As they journeyed on Philip met his friend
Nathaniel, who was a scribe or Doctor of the Law,
that is to say, one well versed in the law of the
Jewish people, and he said to him: "We have found
him of whom Moses in the law and the prophets
did write, Jesus the Son of Joseph of Nazareth."
And Nathaniel said to him: "Can anything good
come from Nazareth?" Philip's only reply was in
the words our Lord had addressed to him: "Come
and see!"

Louis: Why did Nathaniel say that about
Nazareth?

Grandma: Because it was the opinion of the
learned men of Jerusalem that no prophet would

come from the obscure town of Nazareth; and, moreover Nathaniel knew that the Messias was to be born in Bethlehem, and thinking that Nazareth was the birthplace as well as the home of Jesus, he judged he could not be the Messias as Philip announced. However, Nathaniel followed Philip and went to the Savior.

When Jesus saw Nathaniel coming he said of him: "Behold an Israelite indeed in whom there is no guile." Nathaniel, greatly surprised that Jesus should know him, asked: "Whence knowest thou me?" Jesus answered: "Before that Philip called thee, when thou wast under the fig tree, I saw thee." Now, Nathaniel knew that Jesus could not have seen him except by a miraculous power at the distance referred to; he therefore recognized Jesus at once as the Lord, and exclaimed with admiration: "Thou art the Son of God; thou art the King of Israel!" Jesus answered and said to him: "Because I said unto thee: I saw thee under the fig tree, thou believest; greater things than these shalt thou see; . . . thou shalt see the heaven opened and the angels of God ascending and descending upon the Son of Man."

Mary: Why does our Lord say: "The Son of Man?" Who was the Son of Man?

Grandma: Our Lord often spoke of himself as the Son of Man. First, in order to teach us humility, by reminding us that God had so lowered himself as to become man, and also to remind us that he was as truly man as he was truly God. To believe in Christ Jesus, is to believe that the Son of Man is the Son of God. It is to adore God made Man.

This Nathaniel, whom Philip brought to Jesus, is known as the Apostle Bartholomew.

CHAPTER XIII.

THE MARRIAGE FEAST AT CANA.

Three days after our Lord and his disciples journeyed on to Cana, a little town in Galilee, to a wedding feast, to which he and his mother had been invited. Towards the end of the feast the wine gave out. The head steward told Mary, and she approached her Son and said to him: "They have no wine;" and Jesus answered: "Woman, what is it to me and to thee? My hour is not yet come."

Henrietta: Why did our Lord address his mother as woman and answer her thus?

Grandma: This answer was not a reproach, but remember that in Jesus there were two different natures. Jesus was the Son of God before being the Son of the Blessed Virgin Mary; he was God made Man.

As her Son, Jesus was obedient to Mary's every wish; but as God he only obeyed the dictates and guidance of his Heavenly Father; and up to this time he had performed no miracles in public; as he said: "My hour is not yet come."

However, at his mother's request, Jesus performed his first miracle. The Blessed Mother was so certain of the consent of her Son that, untroubled by his reply, she turned to the steward and waiters and said to them: "Whatsoever he shall say to you, do ye." There were standing there six waterjars of stone to be filled, which would serve for the ablutions or purification of the Jews.

Henrietta: What are purifications?

Grandma: It was the custom of the Jews to wash mouth and hands before meals and after meals, and their feet as they came in, and even the feet of strangers and guests who entered a house. Therefore, standing ready were six jars. Jesus said to the waiters: "Fill the water pots with water." And they filled them up to the brim. And Jesus saith to them: "Draw out now, and carry to the chief steward of the feast." And they carried to him what they had drawn. When the steward tasted this water made wine, not knowing whence this delicious wine had come, he went to the bridegroom and said to him: "What have you done? Every man at first setteth forth good wine; and when men have well drunk, then, that which is worse; but thou hast kept the good wine until now." The master of the house could not understand what his steward said to him, because he did not know of the miracle of Jesus; but the steward and waiters who had seen the miracle told every one what they had seen. This was the first public miracle of Jesus, and it increased the faith of his disciples.

Henry: Grandma, why do you say "public miracle;" had Jesus performed miracles privately?

Grandma: The Gospels do not speak of any, but tradition and the accounts of early writers lead us to believe that Jesus had performed miracles from his birth, before he manifested his power to the world at Cana of Galilee.

CHAPTER XIV.

THE HUCKSTERS DRIVEN FROM THE TEMPLE

As the Feast of the Passover was drawning near, Jesus went to Jerusalem for its celebration. As he entered the Temple he found, in the court of the sacred edifice, merchants selling doves and lambs, and money changers seated at their tables prepared to change silver and gold. Indignant at this profanation of his Father's house, Jesus made a whip of cords and drove out the buyers and sellers from the Temple, and he overthrew the tables of the money changers and spilt their money on the floor; and he said: "Take these things hence, and make not the house of my Father a house of traffic."

The Jews, greatly angered at this action of Jesus, said to him: "What sign dost shou show unto us, seeing thou dost these things?" They questioned his right to exercise such authority. Jesus answered: "Destroy this temple, and in three days I will raise it up." The Jews failed to understand that Jesus was not speaking of the Temple which Solomon had built, but of the temple of his body which would be rebuilt, that is, would be resuscitated, three days after the Jews would have put him to death.

After his resurrection his disciples remembered these words.

While Jesus was in Jerusalem, he performed many miracles, and many believed in him; but Jesus, who could read the thoughts of men, did not trust them, for he knew these same Jews would put him to death most cruelly in a few years. Jesus left Jerusalem to traverse Judea, where he remained some time baptizing and preaching. John the Baptist was also baptizing, but on the other side of the Jordan. John's disciples grew jealous of the honor paid to Christ and sought him one day and said to him: "Master, he that was with thee beyond the Jordan, to whom thou gavest testimony, behold he baptizeth and all men come to him."

John answered and said: "A man cannot receive anything unless it be given him from heaven. You yourselves do bear me witness that I said: 'I am not the Christ, but that I am sent before him;' " and John went on in a beautiful discourse, telling them that he was only the servant and friend of Jesus, who was the Lord and Master, and that they must follow Jesus and leave him, and that if they did so at his word, he would rejoice greatly, for he was only the fore-runner of Christ, the Messias.

Jesus, knowing that the Jews and Pharisees were jealous of his power over the hearts of men and saw with vexation the number of disciples who came to him, left Judea and retired into Galilee.

CHAPTER XV.

THE SAMARITAN; OR, JESUS AT JACOB'S WELL.

In order to reach Galilee Jesus and his disciples had to pass through Samaria. As they neared the city of Sichem, which lay surrounded by fertile fields, tired after their long journey on foot, they stopped to rest near Jacob's well.

Louise: Why was it called Jacob's well?

Grandma: Because Jacob had dug and built this well, and he had lived nearby. These very fields he had given to his son, Joseph, who was sold by his brethern, of which we read in the Old Testament.

While his disciples went into the city to buy provisions, Jesus, being very weary, sat on the edge of the well to rest. A woman of Samaria approached to draw water from the well, and Jesus said to her: "Give me to drink."

The woman answered: "How dost thou, being a Jew, ask of me to drink, who am a Samaritan woman?" This she said because there was great hatred between the Jews and the people of Samaria.

Jesus answered and said to her: "If thou didst know the gift of God, and who he is that saith to thee, give me to drink, thou perhaps wouldst have asked of him, and he would have given thee, living water."

The Smaritan woman, greatly surprised, said to Jesus: "Sir, thou hast nothing wherein to draw, and the well is deep; from whence, then, hast thou living water? Art thou greater than our father Jacob, who gave us this well, and drank thereof himself, and his children, and his cattle?"

Jesus answered and said to her: "Whosoever drinketh of this water, shall thirst again; but he that shall drink of the water that I shall give him, shall not thirst forever."

The Samaritan woman, perceiving that Jesus was not an ordinary man, said to him: "Sir, give me this water, that I may not thirst, nor come hither to draw."

Jesus said to her: "Go, call thy husband, and come hither."

"I have no husband," answered the woman.

"Thou hast said well, I have no husband," answered our Lord, "for thou hast five husbands; and he whom thou now hast, is not thy husband. This thou hast said truly."

The Samaritan woman, amazed to see her sins thus known and laid bare by Jesus, said to him: "Sir, I perceive thou art a prophet. . . . I know that the Messias cometh (who is called Christ); therefore, when he is come, he will tell us all things."

Jesus saith to her: "I am he who am speaking with thee."

At that moment the disciples returned from their errand in the city, and were surprised to find Jesus talking with a woman. The woman left there her jar of water and went in great haste into the city and told the people of her meeting with Jesus. "Come," she said, "and see a man who has told me all things whatsoever I have done. Is he not the Christ?" Many followed the woman to Jacob's well.

In the meanwhile his disciples urged Jesus to eat what they had brought. "Master, eat," they prayed him; but he said to them: "I have meat to eat, which you know not."

The disciples, surprised, said to one another: "Hath any man brought him to eat?"

Jesus, who knew what they were whispering, said to them: "My meat is to do the will of him that sent me, that I may perfect his work."

The people of Samaria believed in Jesus on the word of the woman, and when they came to Jesus they begged him to remain with them. He consented to their appeal and remained for two days; and after hearing him, many more believed in him, and they said to the woman: "We now believe, not for thy saying; for we ourselves have heard him and know that this is, indeed, the Savior of the world."

CHAPTER XVI.

JESUS TEACHES IN THE SYNAGOGUE.

Grandma: After two days spent among the Samaritans, Jesus resumed his journeyings to preach in Galilee.

At this time Herod imprisoned John the Baptist, because John reproached him for the wicked life he was leading and for the many evil deeds of his past life.

The first city of Galilee into which Jesus entered was the City of Nazareth, the city where he had lived so long with his mother and Joseph. On the Sabbath day Jesus entered the synagogue.

Louis: What was a synagogue?

Grandma: The synagogue was like our church, a house of prayer, a building where the Jews gathered on the Sabbath day to worship God and read the Scriptures.

Louis: What was the Sabbath day?

Grandma: This was the seventh day of the week, which day the Jews kept, or celebrated, in the same manner as we do Sunday. It was a day of prayer and rest.

Grandma: As I was telling you, Jesus entered the synagogue on the Sabbath day, and taking up one of the books of the Prophet Isaias, he began to read to the assembled people, and explain to them the Scriptures in such a wonderful manner and with such clearness that all gazed upon him in surprise and admiration.

When he had finished reading and explaining they said to one another: "Is not this the son of Joseph, the carpenter?" And they wondered greatly at his wisdom and his knowledge. But when Jesus began to speak to them of their blindness of heart, and to reproach them because they did not believe in him who had lived among them, they grew very angry, and rising up they drove Jesus out of the synagogue and out of the city to the top of the mountain on which their town was built.

They thought to thrust him over this height and kill him, but Jesus miraculously passed through the crowd and "went on his way."

Jack: How was it that the Jews let Jesus escape when they wanted to kill him?

Grandma: Because, by his almighty power, our Lord made himself invisible to the angry crowd around him.

Madeleine: Why did they not believe in our Lord, since they had witnessed his many miracles?

Grandma: Because they did not wish to believe. Their pride revolted at the thought that they would have to recognize as their master and God, a poor carpenter, without fortune, without glory, lacking in all that they expected from the Messias. The Messias, they thought, would help them to conquer the other nations of the earth, and make them, the Jews, the rulers of the world.

However, there were some faithful ones in Nazareth who believed in him.

CHAPTER XVII.

JESUS HEALS THE SON OF THE RULER.

Grandma: Leaving the ungrateful City of Nazareth, Jesus proceeded to Capernaum, where he preached to the people penance and forgiveness of sins, and announced that the kingdom of heaven was at hand. Leaving Capernaum, Jesus journeyed to a city near by, called Cana of Galilee. Here there hastened to him an officer whose son lay ill at Capernaum, and who, learning that Jesus had arrived, found him and begged him to cure his son, who lay ill unto death.

In answer to his prayer, Jesus said: "Unless you see signs and wonders, you believe not."

But the officer besought him the more earnestly to cure his beloved son, saying: "Lord, come down before my poor little one dies."

Then our Lord, pitying his sorrow, said to him: "Go thy way; thy son liveth." The man believed the word which Jesus said to him, and went his way.

The next day as the officer drew near his home, the servants met him and announced to him that his son lived. Immediately he asked at what hour the boy grew better. "Yesterday," they replied, "at the seventh hour the fever left him."

The father knew, then, that it was at the very same hour that Jesus had said to him: "Thy son liveth;" and he believed in our Lord, he, and all his household.

CHAPTER XVIII.

JESUS CALLS PETER AND ANDREW.

Grandma: Jesus continued journeying in Galilee, following the shores of the sea.

Henrietta: On what sea was the shore of Galilee?

Grandma: On the borders of the Mediterranean, to the west, but, on the opposite side, to the east, lay another sea, the Lake of Tiberias. This lake was so large that it was called the sea of Galilee. It was on the shores of this sea that Jesus met Simon, whom he afterwards surnamed Peter, and Andrew his brother.

These men were casting their nets in the sea, for they were fishermen, and Jesus said to them; "Follow me." "And they immediately, leaving their nets, followed him;" proving thus to our Lord, by their prompt obedience to his call, that they believed in him and were eager to consecrate to him their time and their life.

Going a little further, our Lord saw in a boat James, the son of Zebedee, and John, his brother, mending their nets, for they, too, were fishermen. Jesus called them, and at once, "leaving their nets and their father, Zebedee, in the ship with his hired men, they followed him."

Jane: And they left their father?

Grandma: They left their father to obey the call of their Lord and Master to his service.   They should be to us an example of the ready and prompt obedience with which we should always follow the will of God.

CHAPTER XIX.

JESUS CURES THE DEMONIAC.

Grandma: In the company of his disciples, Jesus journeyed to Capernaum. On the Sabbath day he taught in the synagogue, and spoke with such power and wisdom that all were in amazement at his teaching. That day there was in the synagogue a poor, wretched man possessed of the devil, who, seeing Jesus, uttered a great cry, saying: "Let us alone; what have we to do with thee, Jesus of Nazareth? Art thou come to destroy us?" "I know thee who Thou art, the Holy One of God."

Jesus threatened the devil, who spoke through the mouth of this man, and said to him: "Speak no more, and go out of the man."

And the evil one, having thrown the man upon the ground, went out of him, and the man was cured.

Every one was frightened and in consternation, and they said to one another: "What does this mean; he commands even the devils and they obey him?" And the fame of Jesus spread all over the country.

Jesus performed many other miracles in Capernaum. Peter's mother-in-law was ill with a fever and Jesus, taking her by the hand, commanded the fever to leave her. She rose from her bed cured, and served Jesus and his disciples their noonday meal.

After sunset, in the cool of the evening, a crowd of sick people came, or were brought by others, to Jesus to be cured by him; "and laying his hands on every one of them, he healed them." At his word of command, the devils left those whom they possessed, "crying out: . . . Thou art the Son of God." But Jesus forbid the evil spirits to say he was the Christ.

Elizabeth: What does that mean, to be possessed of the devil? Does it mean to be very bad?

Grandma: No; a demoniac, or possessed person, is one whose body is in the possession of the devil, who rules over him and makes him do evil actions, against his will. Such a person is, therefore, not responsible.

Henry: Are persons possessed of the devil nowdays?

Grandma: In countries where our Lord is known and loved it is very rarely seen.

CHAPTER XX.

THE MIRACULOUS DRAUGHT OF FISHES.

Grandma: The next day, at dawn, Jesus left the house and went to a desert place, where he was in the habit of praying alone.

Simon and his other disciples found our Lord, where he had withdrawn to pray, and said to him:

"Every one is looking for you." And Jesus answered: "Let us go into the neighboring towns and cities, that I may preach there also, for to this purpose am I come."

Jesus set out, therefore, to journey through Galilee, teaching in the synagogues and preaching the kingdom of God.

Jack: And what is the kingdom of God?

Grandma: The kingdom of God is heaven, where our Lord dwells and reigns; but it is also the human soul, in which he reigns on earth. Thus each separate soul is his kingdom when we, his creatures, lead a good and holy life, obedient to his law.

Our Lord taught the people how to enter into this kingdom; and he cured their sick and all who were afficted. The good tidings of these cures soon spread over the whole of Syria.

Valentine: How did the news spread in Syria; I thought our Lord was in Galilee?

Grandma: Galilee is in Palestine, and Syria is north of Palestine, quite near. In a short time all Syria knew the miracles of Jesus, and they brought to him their sick and infirm, those who were possessed, who were paralyzed, who were blind, deaf, and dumb; and he cured them all. A great multitude of people followed him wherever he went—people from Galilee and the neighboring countries.

One day on the shores of the lake of Genesareth—

Louis: Where was the lake of Genesareth?

Grandma: The lake of Genesareth was the same as the sea of Tiberias. Genesareth, like Tiberias, was a town built on the shores of the sea of Galilee, to which it gave its name, Tiberias. Our Lord was walking on this shore surrounded by a crowd of people who, eager to hear the word of God, so pressed and crowded around him that, seeing two boats anchored nearby—which the fishermen had left in order to mend their nets—Jesus stepped into Simon Peter's boat and begged him to row out a little from the shore. And sitting in the boat Jesus taught the people.

When he had finished speaking, our Lord said to Simon: "Push out into deeper water. Cast over your nets for the fish."

"Master, Simon answered, we have labored all the night without taking anything, but at your word

I will cast the net." Simon Peter cast his nets, and when he drew them up they were so heavy and full of fishes that the cords of the nets were breaking. He called to his aid the men in the neighboring bark, and when they drew out the nets and landed the fishes, there was such a great quantity that the two barks were filled to overflowing and almost sinking.

Seeing this miracle, Simon Peter threw himself at the feet of Jesus, saying: "Depart from me, O Lord, for I am a sinful man."

Louis: I think Simon Peter was very wrong to speak so to our Lord, who had been so good to him and cured his mother-in-law.

Madeleine: Then Simon Peter was married?

Grandma: Yes; Peter was married and had a daughter named Petronilla; but he left his home and family to follow our Lord. As to what Peter said to Jesus, it was not wrong, as little Louis thinks; on the contrary, it was virtuous. Peter was speaking through humility. This miraculous draught of fishes had revealed to him, more than any miracle before witnessed, that Jesus Christ was God, the Creator of all things, and he did not consider himself worthy to receive him in his poor fisherman's bark. But Jesus said to him:

"Be not afraid; hereafter you shall be fishers of men."

Jack: How could that be; we don't fish for men as we do for fish?

At this the children and even Grandma laughed.

Grandma: By those words our Lord meant that, instead of spending his time in casting his net for fish, Simon Peter was to devote his life to preaching and teaching the people what they should believe and know, and that in this way he would draw men away from the power of the evil one to give them to the service of God.

Simon Peter and James and John, the son of Zebedee, who were with Simon, rowed back to the shore; and they left their boats, their oars, their nets, and followed Jesus.

Up to this time they had believed in Jesus and were his disciples, but they were not always with him. They divided their time between him and their families; but now, "leaving all things, they followed Jesus."

CHAPTER XXI.

THE CURING OF THE LEPER.

Grandma: Last month, my children, I told you of many interesting miracles performed by our Lord, especially that of the miraculous draught of fishes.

After this miracle, Jesus continued journeying from town to town, preaching and teaching the Jews the law of God and making himself known to them.   One day, as he entered the city of Galilee, a man covered with leprosy—

Paul: What is leprosy?

Grandma: Leprosy is a disease of the skin; a terrible malady, most painful and most repulsive, and so contagious that the lepers, those afflicted with this disease, were forbidden to live with other people.   They lived together, apart from every one, outside of the city gates, and were not allowed to touch or even draw near to those in health.   What these poor afflicted ones required for their food and clothing was left where they could find it, but they never communicated with their friends and families.

Jesus, seeing this poor leper standing at a distance, not daring to draw near, but kneeling before him, his face on the ground, saying: "Lord, if thou

wilt, thou canst make me clean," was moved with
pity. "Stretching forth his hand, Jesus touched
him, saying: I will, be thou cleansed." And
immediately the leprosy departed from him and he
was cured. "Jesus said to him: See thou tell no
man; but go, show thyself to the priest, and offer
the gift which Moses commanded." This our Lord
told him to do, that he might show his gratitude and
prove to the priest beyond a doubt that he was
healed of his disease.

As soon as the man left Jesus, he began to publish
far and wide the miracle wrought on him, so that
it began to be known everywhere, and Jesus could
not show himself in that city without being surrounded by a crowd of people, coming from all parts of
the country to be cured by him and to hear him.
But Jesus tried to avoid the crowd, and withdrew
into the desert to pray.

Jack: Why did Jesus forbid the leper to tell of
his cure?

Grandma: To give us an example of humility;
to show us we must not seek praise and honor, and
also because Jesus wished to continue his work of
preaching and healing quietly without commotion.
Jesus knew that if his fame spread over the country,
the High Priests and Pharisees would seek his death,
and though he had come on this earth to die for man's
redemption, his mission here on earth was not yet
accomplished.

Henrietta: Grandma, what does redemption, or to redeem, mean?

Grandma: To redeem means to buy back, to purchase.

Our first parents, Adam and Eve, fell into sin and so fell into the power of the evil one, and through them all their descendants, that is all men, are born slaves of sin.

Jesus by his **sufferings and death** redeemed us, bought us back at the price of his blood, from the power of Satan, and thus gave us all the possibility of being eternally happy with him in the kingdom of heaven, if we follow his law while on earth.

Henrietta: I think I understand. It is as if I were a king, and one of my subjects owed me some money. He refuses to pay , so I put him in prison— him and his whole family; but my son is grieved and pays the debt, and so I open the prison door and the man and his family are free.

Grandma: That was very well explained. I have only one thing to add. The king would say to his subject: The door is open, you are free; but if you do not leave your prison, the door will be closed again for all time and you will be a prisoner eternally. According to Henrietta's example, man's debt is sin; the king is the good God; the prison is this life of trial and sufferings and no hope of eternal salvation; the son is Jesus Christ, our Savior, who pays our debt by his death, and the door of **our** prison is opened; we may enter heaven if we will leave sin. If we will not leave the slavery of sin while on this earth, the door of the prison will be shut, and we shall not enter the kingdom of heaven but remain in hell, prisoners of satan for all eternity

CHAPTER XXII.

THE CALLING OF MATTHEW.

Jesus continued teaching the people who came in crowds to hear him. One day, as he was passing in the street, "he saw a man sitting in the custom-house named Matthew." He was the collector of taxes.

Henrietta: What are taxes?

Grandma: The taxes were charges of money imposed upon the Jews by the Romans, which they were obliged to pay their governor. Jesus said to Matthew: "Follow me. And leaving all things, he rose up and followed him." St. Matthew joined the band of the followers of Jesus and never left him, and later in life wrote the story of Jesus which I am now relating to you.

Henrietta: I thought St. John wrote the life of our Lord.

Grandma: St. John also wrote the life of Christ— or the Gospel as it is called — as did St. Luke and St. Mark. All four accounts of the life of Jesus have been carefully preserved. What one relates is, sometimes, not told by the others; but they all wrote what they had seen or heard, or what others told who had witnessed the life of Christ. They wrote under the guidance of the Spirit of God, who spoke to them interiorly.

Matthew or Levi, for he is known under both names, gave a great feast to Jesus in his own house.

There was at this festival a large number of publicans. This angered the Pharisees and Scribes who were also invited, because they thought themselves superior to the publicans, and they murmured saying to the disciples; "Why do you eat and drink with publicans and sinners?"

"Jesus hearing this, said to them: They that are well have no need of a physician, but they that are sick, for I came not to call the just, but sinners."

John: I don't understand what our Lord meant.

Grandma: Our Lord meant that if the publicans were ill of soul, that is to say, if they were wicked, he came on this earth for them especially; to cure them, and to make them good and pure. Just as a physician does not take care of those who are well, but of those who are ill.

He gave them to understand that he had come to forgive, not to punish. He had come upon this earth, not only for the good and just who followed his law, but also to draw to himself the sinners of the whole world.

CHAPTER XXIII.

THE HEALING OF THE PARALYTIC.

A few days later Jesus returned to Capernaum, the city which he had chosen as his dwelling place. As soon as the people heard in which house he dwelt, they came in crowds to hear him.

So great was the multitude that the house could not hold the people and they crowded around the door-way. Among the crowd were many Pharisees and doctors of the law, from every part of Galilee, from Judea, and even Jerusalem, to hear our Lord, and, if possible, find fault with his speech and bear witness against him.

Jack: What fault could they find with Jesus, who was doing good to all and harming no one.

Grandma: They failed, indeed, to find any fault in our Lord; and this angered them, for they sought every means to accuse him before the Roman governor. Jesus often reproached them for their pride, harshness, and hypocrisy, which increased their anger.

One day, when our Lord was addressing this multitude, "they brought to him a man sick of the palsy, lying on a bed, carried by four men." The crowd was so great they could not enter the house to approach Jesus and lay before him their burden, but full of hope and faith, they would not be turned back. "They went up upon the roof, and opening it they let him down through the tiles with his bed," right in the midst of the crowd at the feet of Jesus.

Louis: What! they were allowed to tear down the roof?

Grandma: In that country the houses are only one story high and the roofs are flat and made of large tiles, one laid beside the other, so that a portion of the roof could easily be uncovered without destroying the house.

"Jesus, seeing their faith, said to the man sick of the palsy: Be of good heart, son, thy sins are forgiven thee."

Then the Pharisees and scribes said to one another "Why doth this man speak thus? He blasphemeth. Who can forgive sins but God alone?" "And Jesus, seeing their thoughts, said: Why do you think evil in your hearts?"

"Which is easier, to say: Thy sins are forgiven thee, or to say: Arise and walk?" "But that you may know that the Son of Man hath power on earth to forgive sins; then said he to the man sick of the palsy: Arise, take up thy bed, and go into thy house."

"And immediately he arose, and taking up his bed went his way in the sight of all."

The crowd was greatly astonished at this great miracle, "and glorified God saying: We never saw the like."

Jane: Grandma, you say the Pharisees accused Jesus of blaspheming. What does that mean, to blaspheme?

Grandma: To blaspheme is to say irreverent things; things that are disrespectful to God and against holy things.

Jack: Jesus had said nothing disrespectful to God.

Grandma: Most certainly not, but in performing this miracle, he had also forgiven the sick man his sins. God alone, as you know, can forgive sin, as the Pharisees said. Our Lord's words plainly said to them: I am God, therefore I forgive sin and cure this man. The Pharisees could not endure the thought that Jesus should be recognized as God, and that he should prove his divinity by his miracles. They wanted a Messias who would be a king, powerful and glorious, who would subject the whole world to the Jewish nation. They refused to believe that Christ was the Son of God, with the power of God to forgive men their sins.

THIRD BOOK

Second Year of the Ministry of Jesus

CHAPTER XXIV.

SECOND YEAR OF THE MINISTRY OF JESUS. THE POOL OF BETHESDA.

Grandma: A short while afterwards Jesus came to Jerusalem for the festival season. At Jerusalem there is a pool of water called Bethesda, which name means "The House of Mercy."

This pond was surrounded on all sides by porches where lay a crowd of sick, infirm, and cripples, who came here to be healed. "An angel of the Lord descended at certain times into the pond, and the water was moved." And he that went down first into the pool after the motion of the water was cured of his disease.

Among these sick people was a poor paralyzed man who had been helpless for thirty-nine years. Jesus seeing him lying upon the ground, and knowing he had been a cripple for so long a time, had pity on him and said to him: "Wilt thou be made whole?" The infirm man answered him: "Sir, I have no man when the water is troubled to put me into the pond. For whilst I am coming, another goeth down before me." Jesus saith to him: "Arise take up thy bed and walk. And immediately the man was made whole; and he took up his bed and walked." "And it was the Sabbath that day.' "The Jews, therefore, said to him that was healed: It is the Sabbath, it is not lawful for thee to take up thy bed."

Jack: How foolish those Jews were. Why did they not allow the poor man to carry his bed?

Grandma: Because, according to the Jewish law, it was forbidden to carry burdens on the Sabbath day.

The paralytic answered. "He that made me whole he said to me: Take up thy bed and walk."

The Jews asked him, therefore: "Who is that man who said to thee: Take up thy bed and walk?"

"But he who was healed knew not who it was," for Jesus, after curing the man, had slipped away from the crowd unnoticed.

Shortly after this Jesus found this man in the Temple, where he had doubtless gone to return thanks, and Jesus said to him: "Behold thou art made whole; sin no more, lest some worse thing happen to thee." Then the man went to the Jews and told them that it was Jesus who had cured him.

Instead of recognizing from all these miracles that Jesus was the promised Messias, who was to save all men, the Jews persecuted him because he healed on the Sabbath day, and because he declared himself the Son of God, equal to God, and God himself, they sought to put him to death.

"'Then Jesus said to them: Amen, amen, I say unto you, the Son cannot do anything of himself, but what he seeth the Father doing, for what things soever he doth, the Son also doth in like manner." "For as the Father raiseth up the dead and giveth life, so the Son also giveth life to whom he will. For neither doth the Father judge any man, but hath given all judgement to the Son, that all men may honor the Father. He who honoreth not the Son honoreth not the Father who hath sent him." "Amen, amen, I say unto you, that he who heareth my word, and believeth him that sent me, hath life everlasting."

Elizabeth: How beautiful are these words of our Lord, yet I do not understand them all.

Grandma: No one understands them fully, they are divine words which express many things we cannot comprehend. But what we can *all* understand is this: That our Lord here declared before all men his divinity. He told them plainly that they must believe he was the Son of God, equal to the Father, and that they did not know the true God when they refused to believe in him, Christ Jesus, who had come upon this earth, and who was true God and true man. Jesus continued saying to them many beautiful things, that he might convince them that he was truly God made man. And he told them that he spoke not for his own glory, but for the glory of God, his Father, and the happiness and salvation of all men.

But the Jews were as if deaf and blind, they would not believe his words nor his miracles, and they continued to seek occasions to find him in fault and to put him to death.

Valentine: We would never have been that wicked.

Grandma: Oh, yes; there are millions of people to-day who act as they did nineteen hundred years ago. To-day God made man is not persecuted, because he is no longer visibly here on earth; but Christ is insulted by words and deeds which are against his law. Men crucify him anew by their evil will and base thoughts and desires, and by actions that are sinful.

How often in the past, and even to-day, do we not find men persecuting the disciples of Christ, the priests; his faithful servants, the Christians; and even his representative on earth, our Holy Father, the Pope. And we ourselves, my children, when we fail to do our duty, we insult our dear Lord and act as did the Jews who so ill-treated him.

Little Louis: Oh, my, my; I certainly am sorry I ever was bad.   I shall try and be good always.

Grandma: Yes, my dear little children, let us all resolve not to be like them, but let us be always full of love and gratitude towards the good Lord Jesus and serve him faithfully all the days of our life.

CHAPTER XXV.

THE MAN WITH THE WITHERED HAND.

Grandma: To-day I have to relate to you another iracle performed by Jesus. One day our Lord tered the synagogue and began to teach the ople. Standing near him was a man who had a thered hand; an affliction caused by some illness by an accident.

The Doctors of the Law and the Pharisees who :re, as I told you, always seeking occasion to accuse sus, watched our Lord sharply to see if he would al this man on the Sabbath day. But Jesus, ıowing their thoughts, said to them: "What man all there be among you that hath one sheep, and the same fall into a pit on the Sabbath day, will not take hold on him and lift it up?"

"Therefore, it is lawful to do a good deed on the bbath day." Then he told the man who had the thered hand to stand up in the midst of them all, d turning to the Pharisees and Doctors of the Law said to them: "It is lawful to do good on the bbath day, or to do evil; to save life, or to destroy?" They dared not reply a word; then Jesus looked them with indignation, and saddened at the blindness of their hearts, he said to the afflicted man: "Stretch forth thy hand, and he stretched it forth and his hand was restored unto him."

The Pharisees were very angry, but they dared not blame him before the people, and going out of the synagogue they consulted together how they might have him put to death.

Little Louis: Grandma, what does blindness of heart mean? How can a heart be blind, when it has no eyes?

Grandma: This does not mean literally that the heart can't see. We say "blindness of heart" to express the evil feelings of the heart, which blind it or prevent it from seeing or understanding the evil that we do.

Henrietta: Don't you know, Louis, when any one says to you: "You see you are wrong," you don't see with your eyes, but you *feel* you are wrong.

Little Louis: Oh, yes; now I understand.

CHAPTER XXVI.

JESUS CHOOSES HIS TWELVE APOSTLES.

Grandma: After this miracle, our Lord with-drew on a mountain nearby, where he spent the night in prayer, as he was accustomed to do often.

Louis: Why did our Lord pray? To whom did he pray, since he was God and all powerful?

Grandma: It is true that he was God, but he was God made man. Do not forget that he had come upon this earth in the form of a man in order that his whole life on this earth might be an example to us. As a man he prayed and honored his Father, to show us how we should pray and worship God, our Father in heaven.

Moreover, our Lord, true God and true man, prayed in very truth as we pray. He adored his Father kneeling and his hands clasped even as we do. Christ worshipped and prayed for the needs of the whole world, and his prayer was more perfect and beautiful than we can understand.

Having prayed all night, when day dawned, Jesus called his disciples to him and "from among them he chose out twelve, to whom he gave the name of Apostles."

Jane: What are Apostles?

Grandma: Apostle means "one sent." Jesus called them thus, because he was to send them into other countries, to other nations, to preach his commandments and to make known his coming. These twelve Apostles were: Simon, whom Jesus surnamed Peter, James, the Son of Zebedee, and John his brother, Andrew, Matthew, Jude, Philip, Thomas, Simon the Cananean, Bartholomew, James, the son of Alpheus, and Judas Iscariot, who betrayed him.

Henry: Since he was to betray him, why did our Lord choose him for an Apostle?

Grandma: When our Lord called him to be an Apostle, Judas was good and full of zeal. He grew wicked later on, because he neglected the favors and graces Christ showered upon him. He loved riches, and became mean and selfish. In choosing him our Lord showed us that even the best among us must watch and fight our evil inclinations, lest we become wicked like Judas Iscariot.

CHAPTER XXVII.

THE SERMON ON THE MOUNT.

Grandma: It was springtime in Judea; the lilies were blooming in the fields, the vines and the fig trees were green upon the hills, and the birds were singing. A great crowd had followed Jesus, and seating himself upon the hilltop, while the people crowded in the plain, some sitting on the grass, some standing, he spoke to them in a beautiful discourse, which is known as "the Sermon on the Mount." I shall tell you some of the beautiful things Christ spoke to this multitude: "Blessed," he said, "are the poor in spirit; for theirs is the kingdom of heaven."

Henrietta: What does poor in spirit mean?

Grandma: The poor in spirit are those who do not seek for greater wealth and gain, and who do not set their hearts and mind on riches, and wish all power for themselves. "Blessed are they that weep; for they shall be comforted." By these words our Lord means that they will be comforted who patiently and with courage bear the sorrows and trials of this life. "Blessed are the meek; for they shall possess the land."

Paul: What land—all the earth?

Grandma: Jesus here promises heaven, the land promised to the good, and also that, in this world, gentleness and meekness will be rewarded by the love that they always inspire. For the gentle and meek win the hearts of the people of all lands, and soften even the hearts of the wicked.

Jesus continued: "Blessed are they that hunger and thirst after justice; for they shall have their fill."

Henrietta: What means to hunger and thirst after justice?

Grandma: This means to desire justice as ardently as we desire to eat and to drink when we are hungry and thirsty. Justice is all that is right and good in the sight of God.

"Blessed are the merciful; for they shall obtain mercy." To be merciful means to forgive. They are blessed who forgive readily all injuries, and who have compassion on the unfortunate, and who comfort and console the afflicted.

"Blessed are the pure of heart; for they shall see God."

Paul: What is pure of heart?

Grandma: Pure means clean; they are blessed whose hearts are washed clean of every evil thought and desire. "Blessed are the peacemakers; for they shall be called the children of God." The peacemakers are those who strive to make peace, who avoid disputes and quarrels, and who yield rather than argue.

And now Jesus said: "Blessed are they that suffer persecution for justice' sake; for theirs is the kingdom of heaven." This is the last of the eight beatitudes, as these promises of our Lord, beginning with the word "blessed," are called. Beatitude means happiness, blessedness.

Our Lord added: "Blessed are ye when they shall revile you, and persecute you, and speak all that is evil against you, untruly, for my sake."

Jane: Why does Jesus say "for my sake?"

Grandma: In all ages, through the wickedness of men, many have been called upon to suffer persecution because of Jesus, or for his sake. For example, the martyrs who were cruelly put to death because they would not deny their faith in Jesus Christ as their Lord and God. The souls of these martyrs at their death enter heaven at once, and so they are blessed indeed. And, therefore, Jesus added: "Be glad and rejoice, for your reward is very great in heaven."

Camille: How different our Lord's teaching is from what we hear around us in the world. They are called blessed and happy who have wealth and fine positions and nothing to suffer.

Grandma: And the world would be right, if there was not another life in heaven or in hell. For we Christians know that when we leave this earth there is an eternity waiting for us; therefore, that those things only are good and blessed which prepare our souls for heaven, and that those things, however good they may appear, which lead our souls to evil, are a real misfortune to us. Jesus spoke at great length, but you are too young to understand all he said. Those of you who wish to know more of this beautiful discourse, can read St. Matthew's Gospel, fifth, sixth, and seventh chapters. What you can understand I shall tell you in our Lord's words.

"Woe to you that are rich, for you have your consolation."

"Woe to you that are filled, for you shall hunger."

Jack: Does our Lord mean we should not be rich, nor eat, nor drink?

Grandma: We may be wealthy, but we must not love riches so much that we keep our wealth for ourselves only. We must share our good things with the needy. Neither must we be greedy, eager for dainty food, while we refuse bread to the poor. If we do, we shall have to suffer in the other world to atone and expiate our gluttony and avarice.

Our Lord continued speaking to the people who surrounded him: "You have heard that it was said to them of old: Thou shalt not kill; and whosoever shall kill shall be in danger of the judgment. But I say to you that whosoever is angry with his brother shall be in danger of the judgment. And whosoever shall say to his brother, Raca, shall be in danger of the council. And whosoever shall say, Thou fool, shall be in danger of hell fire."

Louis: Is Raca a very bad word?

Grandma: Raca was an expression of great contempt. Our Lord desires to show us plainly how wrong it is to abuse others; to despise and to be angry with them.

Little Louis: Our Lord says we must not abuse our brothers, but I suppose it is not wrong to quarrel with our cousins.

Grandma: Oh, yes; for our Lord, in saying brother, means all men—for we are all brothers, because God is Father to us all. The poorest man is your brother, for, like you, he is a child of God and a brother of Christ Jesus.

Jesus added: "If, therefore, thou offer thy gift at the alter, and there thou remember that thy brother hath anything against thee, leave there thy offering before the alter, and go first to be reconciled to thy brother; and then coming thou shalt offer thy gift." "If thy right eye scandalize thee, pluck it out and cast it from thee; and if thy right hand scandalize thee, cut it off and cast it from thee."

Louis: This seems to me very hard to obey.

Grandma: Our Lord does not mean literally that we must tear out our eyes and cut off our hands, but he means that if a thing or a person, to whom we may be as attached as we are to our eyes and hands, should lead us into sin, we must leave it, separate ourselves from it, whatever the separation may cost us. Our Lord often spoke in parables.

Paul: What are parables?

Grandma: A parable means a comparison, a story, which so closely resembles what we wish to teach, that it helps us to make our meaning clear.

Jesus continued. "I say to you do not swear at all, neither by the earth nor by heaven . . . Let your speech be: 'This is so;' 'That is not so;' 'yes;' 'no.' Everything which is more than this comes from an evil source." You have heard that it has been said: "An eye for an eye, a tooth for a tooth."

Jack: What does that mean?

Grandma: In those days revenge was not forbidden by the old Jewish law. If any one injured his neighbor, his enemy rendered him evil for evil injury for injury. Jesus taught a very different law, for he said: "I say to you not to resist evil, but if one strike thee on the right cheek, turn to him also the other. . . . And if a man will take away thy coat, let go thy cloak also. . . . And whosoever will force thee one mile go with him two more."

Elizabeth: Grandma, are we obliged to do all this?

Grandma: These words of our Lord are counsels, advice, not commands. We are obliged to follow the spirit of these counsels, which is to bear injury patiently and to show charity to all men.

Jesus continued. "You have heard: 'Thou shalt love thy neighbor and hate thy enemy. But I say to you: Love your enemies, do good to them that hate you; and pray for them that persecute and calumniate you. That you may be the children of your Father who is in heaven, who maketh the sun to rise upon the good and bad, and raineth upon the just and the unjust." "And if you salute your brethern only, what do you more? Do not the heathen this?" "Be you, therefore, perfect as also your heavenly Father is perfect."

Valentine: What are heathens?

Grandma: Heathens are those who do not know the true God, and who have made for themselves false gods and images of false gods, which they adore instead of the true God. They are also called idolaters, because these images are called idols.

Henrietta: Grandma, Jesus says we must be perfect as God is perfect. We can never be as perfect as he.

Grandma: No; we cannot be as perfect as the good God, but we can and must strive to become perfect; doing always all we can to please God, by taking Jesus Christ as our model.

And, continued Jesus: "Take heed that you do not your justice before men, to be seen by them; otherwise you shall not have a reward of your Father who is in heaven." "Therefore, when thou dost any almsdeed, let not thy left hand know what thy right hand doth."

Louis: How can a hand know or not know what is done? A hand can't think.

Grandma: Our Lord here teaches us that we must not do our good deeds to be seen by men, that they may praise us; for their praise would be our only reward; but to be seen only by our Father in heaven, who will reward us.

CHAPTER XXVIII.

THE "OUR FATHER."

Grandma: And Jesus taught the multitude how they should pray, saying: "And when you pray, you shall not be as hypocrites that love to stand and pray in the synagogues and corners of the streets, that they may be seen by men. Amen I say to you, they have received their reward." "But thou, when thou shalt pray, enter into thy chamber, and having shut the door, pray to thy Father in secret; and thy Father who seeth in secret will repay thee."

Our Lord here warns us again not to do good in order to be seen by men. When we go to church, which is the house of God, we must not go, as the hypocrites do, to be seen. And, continued Jesus: "When you pray, speak not much, as the heathens do." . . . "Thus, therefore, shall you pray: "Our Father who art in heaven, hallowed be thy name. Thy kingdom come. Thy will be done on earth as it is in heaven. Give us this day our daily bread. And forgive us our trespasses, as we forgive those who trespass against us. And lead us

not into temptation. But deliver us from evil.'
Amen."

Jane: But that is the Our Father which we say
every day!

Grandma: Yes, it is the beautiful prayer called
the Our Father, because of these two words with
which it begins.

Jane: I never knew Jesus had made that prayer.

Grandma: Yes, Christ Jesus made the Our
Father to teach how we should pray and what we
should ask of God. It is the most beautiful and
wonderful prayer in the world. It could not be
otherwise, since it was made by God himself. And
to impress upon us the duty of forgiveness, Jesus
added: "If you will forgive men their offences,
your heavenly Father will forgive you also your
offences. But if you will not forgive men, neither
will your Father forgive you your offences." So you
see, children, how good it is that we sometimes have
cause to forgive our neighbor, because by our forgiveness of injuries done to us, we ourselves obtain
mercy from our Father in heaven. And Jesus said:
"Lay not up to yourselves treasurers on earth:
where the rust and moth consume, and where
thieves break through and steal. But lay up for
yourselves treasures in heaven; where neither the
rust nor the moth doth consume, not the thieves
break through, nor steal."

Louis: What treasures must we collect for ourselves?

Grandma: Prayer, almsgiving, acts of charity and humility, and gentleness and obedience, which are treasures in God's sight; the only gifts we can offer him and which no one can take from us. "Therefore," said Jesus, "be not solicitous for your life, what you shall eat, nor for your body, what you shall put on. . . . Behold the birds of the air, for they neither sow, nor do they reap, nor gather into barns; and your heavenly Father feedeth them. Are not you of much more value than they? . . . Be not solicitous therefore, saying: What shall we eat, or what shall we drink, or wherewith shall we be clothed? . . . For your Father knoweth that you need all these things. Seek ye therefore first the kingdom of God and his justice, and all these things shall be added unto you." Here our Lord teaches that while we attend to the business of our daily lives, it must be without worry and anxiety and with confidence and trust in our heavenly Father.

And continued Christ: "Judge not, that you may not be judged. For with what judgement you judge, you shall be judged. . . . And why seest thou the mote that is in thy brother's eye, and seeth not the beam that is in thy own eye?"

Mary Theresa: How could a beam of wood be in any one's eyes?

Grandma: When our Lord speaks of the beam and of the mote, which is the tiniest particle possible he is again using a comparison, a similitude. He here compares the small faults, as small as motes, which we see in others, to the great faults, as large as beams, which we do not see in ourselves; and, therefore, our Lord added: "Thou hpyocrite, cast out first the beam out of thy own eye, and then thou shalt see to cast out the mote out of thy brother's eye." "Ask, and it shall be given you; seek, and you shall find; knock, and it shall be opened to you."

Paul: Grandma, I often ask for things, and I don't get them; and I knock, and I am told I can't come in; and I look for things, and I can't find them. Yesterday I asked you for a knife, and you did not give it to me.

Grandma: Little Paul, you forget that Jesus speaks here to men about the things of God. He tells us to ask God for those things we need, and he will not refuse us, provided what we ask be good and useful to us. But our Father in heaven will refuse to give us what we ask if it be dangerous for us, as I refused you a knife which might have hurt you. And when our Lord speaks of seeking and of knocking, that we may find and that the door may be opened to us, he refers to the kingdom of heaven. This kingdom will be ours if we seek it with perseverance by praying persistently for those virtues which give us a quiet conscience, at peace with God. And this good conscience is a beginning of his kingdom even in this world.

Paul: What is the conscience?

Grandma: Our conscience is that inner voice which tells us what is right and what is wrong, and which warns us that even when alone we are under the eye of our Father in heaven. Conscience is the voice of God.

Jesus said many more beautiful things, and ended his discourse on the Mount with these words:

"Every one therefore that heareth these my words, and doth them, shall be likened to a wise man that built his house upon a rock. And the rain fell, and the floods came, and the winds blew, and they beat on that house, and it fell not, for it was founded on a rock." "And every one that heareth these my words, and doth them not, shall be like a foolish man that built his house upon the sand. And the rain fell, and the floods came, and the winds blew, and they beat upon that house, and it fell, and great was the fall thereof."

The multitude listened with wonder and delight to these words of Christ, for he spoke as one who had power to teach; not as the scribes and Pharisees who had long taught them, but who had failed to win them to the love cf God as did Christ Jesus.

CHAPTER XXIX.

THE CENTURION.

Grandma: After the wonderful sermon of which I told you, Jesus came down from the mountain followed by a great crowd, and returned to Capernaum. A Roman Centurion drawing near said to him—

Jane: What is a Centurion?

Grandma: A Centurion was a Roman officer who had one hundred men under his command. The Centurion said to Jesus: "Lord, my servant lieth at home sick of the palsy, and is grievously tormented." And Jesus said to him: "I will come and heal him."

And the Centurion answered, and said: "Lord I am not worthy that thou shouldst enter under my roof; but only say the word, and my servant shall be healed."

Peter: Why, these are the very same words the priest uses before he receives Holy Communion and before he gives us Holy Communion.

Grandma: Yes; these words so perfect in their humility, have come down to us from this Centurion, and are repeated by the priest at every Mass, and by all who draw near to Jesus in Holy Communion.

And the Centurion added: "For I also am a man under authority; and I say to one. Go, and he goeth; and to another: Come, and he cometh; and to my servant: Do this, and he doth it."

Jesus hearing these words was surprised, and said to them that followed him: "Amen I say to you, I have not found so great faith in Israel. Many shall come from the East and the West, and shall sit down with Abraham and Isaac and Jacob in the kingdom of heaven, but the children of the kingdom shall be cast out into the exterior darkness: there shall be weeping and gnashing of teeth."

Louis: Grandma, I don't quite understand these words—who will come from the East and the West?

Grandma: By these words our Lord praises the Centurion—who was a Roman, not a Jew—and at the same time he teaches the Jews a lesson. He tells them that other nations to the East and to the West of Judea, who had not been blessed as the Jews had been in having Christ, the Savior of the world, with them, will none the less believe in his coming. He adds that they will be saved by their faith as surely as were the Jewish patriarchs, Abraham, Isaac, and Jacob, who are in the kingdom of heaven.

Louis: And who are the children of the kingdom, of whom our Lord speaks, and why will they be cast into darkness?

Grandma: The children of the kingdom were the Jewish people. A nation specially watched over by God, and to whom he sent his only Son, Jesus Christ, that he might teach them the way to the kingdom of God. But they were ungrateful and rebellious sons of God—and refused to believe in him. So our Lord says that, while the other nations of the earth will enter the kingdom of heaven, those who refused to believe in him will be cast into the darkness of hell.

Jane: What a terrible thing is hell.

Grandma: Yes; more terrible than any suffering in this world can be. To avoid this eternal punishment we must do our duty faithfully; we must resist temptation and love God. In a word, we must be good Christians.

And turning to the Centurion, Jesus said: "Go and as thou hast believed, so be it done to thee." "And the servant was healed at the same hour."

CHAPTER XXX.

THE SON OF THE WIDOW OF NAIM.

Grandma: Jesus left Capernaum, and took the road to Naim, in the company of his disciples and followed by a great crowd.

Drawing near to the gates of the city, they met a funeral procession wending its way to the burying ground outside the city.

Carried on a litter by his kindred lay the body of the dead, a young man, "the only son of his mother, and she was a widow."

Jesus, seeing the distress of the poor mother, was moved with pity.

Drawing near, he touched the litter, and the bearers stood still, and Jesus said to the dead: "Young man, I say to thee, arise!" "And he that was dead sat up and began to speak, and Jesus gave him to his mother."

Elizabeth: How wonderful it is that our Lord could raise the dead to life!

Grandma: Jesus raised the dead to life by the the same power that he created. Christ was God as well as man—and it is not more wonderful to restore the dead to life than it is to create a being into life.

And all who witnessed this miracle were filled with fear, "and they glorified God, saying: A great prophet is risen up among us, and God hath visited his people."

CHAPTER XXXI.

JOHN THE BAPTIST SENDS HIS DISCIPLES TO JESUS.

Grandma: Rumors of the miracles of Jesus were spread far and wide in all Judea and in all the neighboring country. John the Baptist heard these things, and calling two of his disciples he sent them to Jesus, bidding them ask Christ who he was; saying: "Art thou he that art to come; or look we for another?"

Henry: Why did not John go himself to Jesus, instead of sending his disciples?

Grandma: John was detained in prison by Herod, and he sent his disciples to witness if this was the Christ, the Messias, whom he had long known.

While these messengers stood by, Jesus healed in their presence "many of their diseases and sores, and evil spirits, and to many that were blind he gave sight;" and turning to the two disciples Jesus said: "Go and relate to John what you have heard and seen: The blind see, the lame walk, the lepers are made clean, the deaf hear, the dead rise again; to the poor the Gospel is preached."

In these words our Lord gave John the Baptist a sign that he was truly the Messias, with the power of God to heal all men; the Christ who had come to preach the Gospel to all, rich and poor alike, which means the message of good tidings of God's kingdom.

When the messengers left with their answer for John the Baptist, our Lord began to speak of John to the people: "What went ye out into the desert to see? a reed shaken with the wind?" . . . "But what went you out to see? a prophet? yea, I say to you, and more than a prophet. This is he of whom it is written: Behold I send my angel before thy face, who shall prepare thy way before thee."

Louis: What means "before thy face;" and whose way did the angel prepare?

Grandma: St. John the Baptist was the angel, the messenger, to whom our Lord refers. He was the forerunner of Christ, sent to foretell, to announce, his coming. Then our Lord reproached the Jews because they had not recognized John as his forerunner, and that they now refused to see in himself Christ the Savior of the World, foretold by John the Baptist.

CHAPTER XXXII.

THE SINFUL WOMAN IN THE HOUSE OF SIMON.

Grandma: And now I shall relate to you an instance of the great mercy of Jesus Christ for all repentant sinners.

One day a Pharisee named Simon invited Jesus and his disciples to a banquet in his house. While they were at table a woman, who was known as one who led a wicked life, came into the banquet-room bearing an alabaster box of precious ointment.

Little Louis: Who was this woman?

Grandma: This woman was Mary Magdalene, the sister of Martha and of Lazarus, who were the friends of Jesus. She was young, rich, and beautiful. She lived in the town of Magdala, spending her life in pleasures and in sin, far from thoughts of God. But she had seen and heard Jesus, and repentance was beginning to stir her soul.

Hearing that he was in the house of Simon, she came to him full of sorrow for her sins. Throwing herself at the feet of Jesus, she kissed his feet, bathed them in the tears she shed, wiped them with her long hair, and breaking her alabaster box, poured its perfume on his feet. Jesus was silent, and the

Pharisee who had invited him to this dinner thought to himself: "If this man were a prophet, he would surely know who and what manner of woman this is that toucheth him; that she is a sinner."

Jesus read the thought of Simon and said to him: "Simon, I have something to say to thee." And Simon answered: "Master, say it." And Jesus said: "A certain creditor had two debtors; the one owed him five hundred pence and the other fifty; and whereas they had not wherewith to pay, he forgave them both. Which, therefore, of the two loveth him most?" Simon answering, said: "I suppose that he to whom he forgave most." And Jesus said to him: "Thou hast judged rightly."

And turning to the woman, he said to Simon: "Dost thou see this woman? I entered into thy house, thou gavest me no water for my feet; but she with tears hath washed my feet, and with her hair hath wiped them. Thou gavest me no kiss; but she, since she came in, hath not ceased to kiss my feet. My head with oil thou didst not anoint; but she with ointment hath anointed my feet. Wherefore I say to thee: Many sins are forgiven her, because she hath loved much. But to whom less is forgiven, he loveth less."

Then, turning to Mary Magdalene, whose face was bathed in tears, he said in a voice full of kindness and of mercy: "Thy sins are forgiven thee."

And those that were at table with Jesus began to say to each other: "Who is this that forgiveth sins also?"

And he said to the woman: "Thy faith hath saved thee, go in peace."

Mary Magdalene ever afterwards led a life of repentance, and we shall find her following Jesus and ministering to him.

Jesus continued to journey through towns and villages, everywhere announcing the glad tidings of salvation, followed by his twelve disciples and by many whom he had delivered of their infirmities.

CHAPTER XXXIII.

MIRACLES AND PARABLES OF JESUS.

Grandma: On one occasion a man born blind and dumb was brought to Jesus, and he cured him, so that the man spoke and saw.

All the people were amazed at this new miracle, and said to each other: "Is not this the son of David?" And they flocked to him to witness his miracles and to hear the words of wisdom, strength, and love which fell from his lips. So great was the crowd that he could not find time to eat and to drink. While he was speaking to this eager multitude, a man pushed his way through the crowd, saying, "Thy mother and thy brethren stand without, seeking thee.'

Louis: I thought our Lord was the only son of the Blessed Virgin Mary?

Grandma: You are quite right: Jesus Christ, the Son of God, was the only child of the Virgin Mary; but in Hebrew, or in the Syrian tongue, which was spoken in Judea, cousins are called brothers. It is so in other countries besides Judea. In Russia, for instance, there is no word for cousin. They say "brother and sister once removed." Looking around

at those who sat with him, Jesus answered this
messenger: "Who is my mother and who are my
brethren? Behold my mother and my brethren.
For whosoever shall do the will of my Father that
is in heaven, he is my brother and sister and mother."

By these words our Lord shows his love for all
men whom he came to save, and especially his love
for those who love God and who obey his law, and
for those who leave riches, honors, pleasures for his
sake. They are to him mother, brother, and sister.

Leaving the house, Jesus took the road leading to
the lake, and seated himself on the shore, but the
multitude was so great that he entered a boat and
pushed out a little from the land. Seated in this
boat the crowd could see him and hear him, and he
taught them in parables.

Henry: What is a parable?

Grandma: As I have already explained, a parable
is a story, a tale, more serious than a fable, which is
related to make a truth clearer or to explain a doctrine. In those days it was customary to teach by
means of fables and parables containing a hidden
meaning.

One of our Lord's parables which he related to
the multitude is as follows: "The sower went out
to sow his seed. And while he soweth, some fell
by the wayside; and it was trodden down, and the
birds of the air ate it up. And some fell upon a
rock; and as soon as it was sprung up it withered

away, because it had no moisture. And some fell among thorns; and the thorns growing up with it, choked it. And some fell upon good ground; and being sprung up, yielded fruit a hundredfold."

Jane: I do not understand this parable.

Grandma: I shall give you the explanation our Lord himself gave his disciples, who did not understand it any better than you do, and they asked: "Why speakest thou to them in parables?

And Jesus answered: "Now the parable is this: The seed is the word of God. And they by the wayside are they that hear; then the devil cometh and taketh the word out of their heart, lest believing they should be saved. Now they upon the rock, are they who. when they hear, receive the word with joy; and these have no roots; for they believe for a while, and in time of temptation they fall away. And that which fell among the thorns, are they who have heard, and going their way, are choked with the cares and riches and pleasures of this life, and yield no fruit. But he that received the seed upon good ground, this is he that heareth the word, and understandeth and beareth fruit and yieldeth the one a hundredfold, and another sixty, and another thirty."

Little Louis: What does that mean, to yield fruit a hundredfold?

Grandma: This means the fruits of the virtues which you practise. For example, you practise the virtue of patience, and you become gentle, amiable, and kindly. These virtues are the fruits of your patience. And so the good seed of the word of God, sown in our hearts, bears fruit which increases if we are faithful in the practice of virtue.

And Jesus spoke to them another parable:

"The kingdom of heaven is likened to a man that sowed good seed in his field. But while men were asleep, his enemy came and oversowed cockle among the wheat and went his way."

Paul: And what is cockle?

Grandma: Cockle is a weed which is frequently found among the wheat, and which is injurious to it.

In this parable the cockle, our Lord tells them, grew up with the good wheat. "Then the servants of the good man of the house, coming, said to him: Sir, didst thou not sow good seed in thy field? Whence, then, hath it cockle? And he said to them: An enemy hath done this. And the servants said to him: Wilt thou that we go and gather it up? And he said: No; lest, perhaps, gathering up the cockle, you root up the wheat also together with it. Suffer both to grow until the harvest, and in the time of the harvest I will say to the reapers: Gather up first the cockle, and bind it into bundles to burn, but the wheat gather ye into my barn."

When our Lord had finished speaking, and had dismissed the multitude, who returned to their own homes, the disciples came to him, asking him to explain the parable of the cockle in the wheat field.

Henrietta: It does not seem to me the Apostles were very clever. They never understand our Lord.

Grandma: The Apostles were, indeed, ignorant men. It was through God's great mercy and grace that they were changed and enlightened at Pentecost, when the Holy Ghost came down upon them, as you will see later. Jesus replied to his disciples: "He that soweth the good seed is the Son of man. And the field is the world. And the good seed are the children of the kingdom. And the cockle are the children of the wicked one. And the enemy that sowed them is the devil. But the harvest is the end of the world. And the reapers are the angels. Even as cockle, therefore, is gathered up, and burnt with fire; so shall it be at the end of the world. The Son of man shall send his angels, and they shall gather out of his kingdom all scandals, and them that work iniquity. And shall cast them into the furnace of fire: there shall be weeping and gnashing of teeth. Then shall the just shine as the sun, in the kingdom of their Father."

Valentine: What means iniquity?

Grandma: Iniquity is evil. Our Lord here tells us that those who do evil, who commit sins, will not enter heaven, but will be cast into hell.

Our Lord gave the multitude another parable to explain the kingdom of heaven. This one you can readily understand:

"The Kingdom of heaven is like to a net cast into the sea, and gathering together all kinds of fishes. Which, when it was filled, they drew out, and sitting by the shore, they chose out the good into vessels, but the bad they cast forth. So shalt it be at the end of the world. The angels shall go out, and shall separate the wicked from among the just. And shall cast them into the furnace of fire: there shall be weeping and gnashing of teeth."

Louis: It seems to me our Lord so often speaks of "weeping and gnashing of teeth."

Grandma: If our merciful Lord often speaks of the punishment of hell, it is in order to impress upon his hearers all the horror of being lost, and to urge them to give up evil and do good, that they may avoid this eternal separation from God.

When our Lord had finished these parables, he said to them: "Have ye understood these things? And they said to him: Yea."

Then our Lord set out to preach in other cities. Seeing how great was the multitude around him, he ordered his disciples to row over to the other side of the Lake of Genesareth.

Then a Doctor of the Law, drawing near, said to him: "Master, I will follow thee withersoever thou shalt go." And Jesus said to him: "The foxes have holes, and the birds of the air nests; but the Son of man hath not where to lay his head." By these words our Lord told the scribes and Doctors of the Law that he had no riches to offer his followers. The life of Christ on earth was a life of poverty. Turning to his disciples our Lord said: "Let us pass over to the other side."

CHAPTER XXXIV.

THE QUIETING OF THE TEMPEST.

Grandma: The disciples, having dismissed the multitude, rowed out into the lake with our Lord on board their boat. Other barks followed. Then there arose a great storm, so great that the waves washed over the little bark, and threatened to engulf it. Jesus seated in the stern, with his head on the pilot's pillow, slept, wearied with the toils of the day.

Little Louis: What is the stern?

Grandma: The stern is the hind part of a ship, the bow is the fore part. Alarmed at the raging of the storm, the disciples wakened Jesus, and said to him in great excitement:

"Master, doth it not concern thee that we perish? And rising up, he rebuked the wind and said to the sea: Peace, be still. And the wind ceased, and there was made a great calm. And he said to them: Why are you fearful? Have ye not faith yet?"

But the disciples were filled with fear and wonder, "and they said to one another: Who is this, think you, that he commandeth both the winds and the sea, and they obey him?"

Henry: What, the disciples did not yet understand that Jesus was the Son of God?

Grandma: They had the knowledge that Christ was the Son of God, but were not yet firm in their belief, and each new miracle that Jesus performed surprised and frightened them. Before and after these miracles, which showed his divine power, they saw our Lord poor, humble, often weary, a man of sorrow, and they failed to realize that the weakness of the Son of man was combined with the power of the Son of God.

CHAPTER XXXV.

THE CURE OF THE MAN POSSESSED OF AN EVIL SPIRIT.

Grandma: After the stilling of the tempest, Jesus and his disciples landed in Gadara on the opposite shore of Galilee.

Hardly had Jesus set foot upon this land, when there came rushing to him a man possessed of an evil spirit, who tormented him sorely. The evil spirit had made this man so violent that he could not be bound, even with iron chains. He dwelt in the caves among the hills, a wild creature, feared and avoided by all the people. Throwing himself at the feet of Christ the wretched demoniac cried out: "What have I to do with thee, Jesus, the Son of the Most High God? I beseech thee do not torment me." And Jesus commanded the evil spirit saying: "Go out of the man, thou unclean spirit."

And Jesus questioned him: "What is thy name?" The evil spirit replied: "My name is Legion; for we are many."

There was on the mountain side a herd of swine feeding, and the evil spirits besought our Lord that they might be permitted to enter into the swine and Jesus permitted it.

"The devils, therefore, went out of the man and entered into the swine; and the herd ran violently down a steep place into the lake, and were drowned." The men who kept these herds were frightened, and they fled to the city and told what had happened.

And the men from the city, and those who owned the swine, "came to Jesus, and they found the man, out of whom the devils had departed, sitting at his feet, clothed, and in his right mind; and they were afraid." And those standing around, who had witnessed the miracle, related what had happened; and these men besought Jesus that he would leave their country.

Jane: How foolish these people are: instead of asking Jesus to stay with them, they beg him to leave!

Grandma: These men of Gadara did what all men do who are not good Christians, and who think only of the goods of this world. They thought only of the loss of their swine. They failed to understand that the presence of our Lord was to them more useful and more profitable than their herds could possibly be.

Louis: I don't see how other men do this.

Grandma: They drive Jesus out of their hearts when they prefer their pride, their greed, their anger, their indolence to his presence within them.

For our Lord cannot dwell in our hearts when we prefer these sins to the practice of the virtues of charity, gentleness, humility, and mortification.

When Jesus embarked to return to Galilee the man whom he had delivered from the power of the evil one, begged to accompany him. The Lord would not permit it, but said to him: "Return to thy house and to thy friends and tell them how God hath done great things for thee, and hath had mercy on thee."

Jack: Why did not our Lord let this poor man go with him?

Grandma: Because our Lord knew that this man would be more useful to the glory of God in his own country, by making known this great miracle, than by joining the company of his disciples. The man, therefore, went his way, and published in all the cities around what Jesus had done for him, "and all men wondered."

CHAPTER XXXVI.

THE DAUGHTER OF JAIRUS.

Grandma: Jesus, having crossed over the Lake of Genesareth to the land, was met by an eager crowd, who had gathered on the shore to greet him. Among the multitude was a chief of the synagogue named Jairus. He ran eagerly to Christ, and throwing himself at his feet, distracted with grief, he poured out his prayer, saying: "My daughter is at the point of death, come, lay thy hand upon her, that she may be safe, and may live."

Moved with pity, Jesus followed Jairus. Behind him, around him, thronged the crowd. In this multitude was a poor woman who had been suffering with a loss of blood for twelve years. She had consulted many physicians, who were unable to cure her. She had spent all her money seeking health, and yet was growing worse rather than better.

Having heard of the miracles of Jesus, she came to him in the crowd unnoticed and touched his garment, for she had said to herself: "If I but touch the hem of his garment, I shall be healed."

And immediately she felt in her body that she was cured of the evil."

No one had noticed her, but Jesus knew that a grace had gone out from him. He turned to the crowd and said: "Who hath touched my garments?" "And his disciples said to him: Thou seest the multitude thronging thee, and sayest thou who hath touched me?" But our Lord looked around the crowd seeking her whom he had healed. The poor woman, ashamed, and full of fear, in spite of her great happiness, meeting the eyes of Christ, fell trembling at his feet, and told before all the people her illness and her cure. Jesus said to her: "Daughter, thy faith hath made thee whole; go in peace, and be thou whole of thy disease."

While he was yet speaking, some of the servants of Jairus came hurrying to him, saying: "Thy daughter is dead; why dost thou trouble the Master any longer?"

But Jesus, having overheard the servant, said to the ruler of the synagogue: "Fear not; only believe, and she shall be safe." And he continued on his way to the house of Jairus. Here he found assembled a great crowd of mourners, wailing and weeping and uttering great cries of distress; for it was customary among the Jews to lament the dead loudly to show their sympathy for the parents of the deceased.

Our Lord said to them: "Why make this ado,

and weep? the damsel is not dead, but sleepeth."
And the mourners mocked him. But Jesus, taking
with him Peter, and James, and John, and the father
and mother of the young girl, went into the darkened
room. Here, ready for burial, lay the body of a
twelve-year-old maiden. Taking her by the hand,
Jesus said to her: "Talitha cumi." Which means:
"Damsel, I say to thee, arise. And immediately
the young girl rose up, and walked."

And Jesus bade them give her something to eat.
All they who had seen this miracle were in admiration and in astonishment, and Jesus forbade them
to tell any one. It was not long, however, before
all the country round knew of this miracle.

Louis: How did people know it, since our Lord
had forbidden them to tell of it?

Grandma: Because, no doubt, in spite of his
prohibition, people spoke of this miracle—some
through admiration, some through indiscertion. In
those days, you see, as to-day, our Lord was not
always obeyed.

CHAPTER XXXVII.

THE CURING OF THE BLIND AND THE DUMB.

Grandma: As Jesus left the house of Jairus two blind men followed him crying out: "Have mercy on us, O Son of David!" When Jesus reached the house where he dwelt they drew near, and Christ, full of pity for their affliction, turned to them and said: "Do you believe that I can do this for you? They said to him: Yea, Lord. Then he touched their eyes, saying: According to your faith, be it done unto you. And their eyes were opened." And Jesus said: "See that no man know this."

But on leaving our Lord, they spread the good news of their cure far and wide.

Jack: And did our Lord punish them?

Grandma: The Gospel does not indicate that our Lord reproached them; and it is more than likely he did not do so.

Jack: I don't understand how it is that Jesus forbids these blind men to tell of their cure, and when they disobey him, they are not punished. Yet, I remember you told us how when Moses disobeyed God by striking the rock *twice*, for the water to gush out, instead of striking it only *once*, as God had commanded him, he was severely punished, and not allowed to enter the promised land.

Grandma: I shall show you the difference between the disobedience of Moses and that of these blind men. Moses disobeyed from the mistrust of God. One blow of his rod seemed to him insufficient, in spite of God's command. Now, the blind men disobeyed through their gratitude and love. They longed to make known to their countrymen the power and goodness of Christ. And in their eagerness they disobeyed. We frequently see such cases of disobedience, and nowhere do we see that our Lord was angry. Our Lord readily forgives a fault that springs from no evil cause, but from zeal ill-directed or unwise.

Seeing the cure of the blind men, they brought to Christ a man possessed of a dumb devil that he might heal him, also.

Paul: What is a dumb devil?

Grandma: It was an evil spirit which possessed the man so that he could not speak. As soon as our Lord had driven out the devil, the man spoke and the people were in admiration and cried out: "Never was the like seen in Israel!"

But the Pharisees, who feared that this miracle would gain many followers to Christ, said to the people that by the aid of the devil he cast out the devils.

Jane: And did the people believe this?

Grandma: No doubt some believed it. For is it not unfortunately true that even in our own days we are more disposed to believe evil than good of others?

CHAPTER XXXVIII.

CHRIST VISITS NAZARETH.

Grandma: Jesus left this neighborhood to journey in Galilee. He went first to his own city of Nazareth, where he had lived with Mary and Joseph through all his childhood and youth. On the Sabbath day he preached in the synagogue. A large number gathered to hear him, and they were amazed at his eloquence and power. And they said to one another: "How came this man by this wisdom and miracles? Is not his mother called Mary, and his brethren James and Joseph and Simon and Jude?"

They referred to his cousins, as I have already explained to you. And they added: "Are not his sisters here amongst us?" In Jesus, whom they knew to be the Son of Mary and Joseph the carpenter, they refused to recognize the Messias. Their pride revolted, and they would not believe he had the power to teach them. "And Jesus said to them: A prophet is not without honor, save in his own country, and in his own house." "And he wrought not many miracles there because of their unbelief."

Valentine: Why did he not perform miracles?

Grandma: Because when our Lord healed the sick and performed miracles on the afflicted in body, he expected and looked for faith in the soul. He looked for sorrow for past sins and purpose of amendment. Here in Nazareth he failed to find these good dispositions; on the contrary, they were unbelieving, and, therefore, after healing a few of their sick, he left his own city, never to return within its ungrateful walls.

But our Lord went into the neighboring cities, preaching everywhere and healing the sick.

CHAPTER XXXIX.

THE MISSION OF THE APOSTLES.

Grandma: Wherever Christ journeyed he found the people as sheep without a shepherd, willing and eager to listen to the word of God, but without teachers to show them the right way. And calling to him his twelve disciples Christ sent them two by two to preach in all that country. He gave them power over the unclean spirits.

Louis: What are unclean spirits?

Grandma: These are the spirits of evil, the demons. Our Lord commanded his disciples to carry with them on their journeyings, "neither staff, nor scrip, nor bread, nor money, nor two coats."

Mary Theresa: And how did these poor Apostles live?

Grandma: They lived on alms. Our Lord did for them what he does everyday for those who devote themselves to his service, and who trust in him. To these, his faithful friends, he inclines the hearts of those who listen to the word of God, of those who desire to know the truth and to do good.

To-day we have the Sisters of Charity; the Little Sisters of the Poor; the Franciscans, and many

others; who, like the Apostles, possess nothing and
live on alms.

Our Lord in thus sending out his Apostles, poor
in all things and depending on charity, gave the first
example of the religious life with its practice of holy
poverty. "And he said to them: Wheresoever
you shall enter into a house, there abide till you
depart from that place. And when you come into
the house salute it, saying: Peace be to this house.
. . . And whosoever shall not receive you, nor
hear your words, going forth from thence, shake
off the dust from your feet."

Henrietta: Why should they shake off the dust
from their feet?

Grandma: This was as a sign of malediction,
the opposite of blessing, or benediction. It was as
if to say: You refuse to receive us, the servants of
God, and you will be punished; and since you refuse
us the bread and shelter we stand in need of, we shall
keep nothing of yours, not even the dust of your
home which has gathered on our feet. To merit
the blessing of God we must be always polite and
charitable to the religious who are God's servants,
and who came to us begging alms in his name for a
church, a school, a convent, a charity. Give little
if you have but little, but do not refuse what is asked
in the name of God, and God's blessing will follow
your charity.

Our Lord added: "Behold I send you as sheep

in the midst of wolves. Be ye, therefore, wise as serpents and simple as doves."

And he told them that they would be persecuted and hated for his sake, that they would be obliged to flee from city to city to preach the kingdom of God. For, said Jesus: "I came not to send peace, but the sword."

Louis: What does that mean?

Grandma: Our Lord here foretells the persecution of his servants. Those whom his disciples converted to Christianity would be persecuted by the unbelievers, tortured, and even put to death for their belief in Christ Jesus.

Our Lord added: "He that receiveth you, receiveth me. . . . And whosoever shall give to drink to one of these little ones a cup of cold water in the name of a disciple, he shall not lose his reward."

The Apostles, therefore, set out according to the orders of the Master. Everywhere they went, they preached repentance for sins, charity towards all men, and love of one another for the sake of Christ. Wherefore, when we Christians give alms we give to Christ Jesus himself. When we give in this spirit, our Lord accepts our charity and rewards us eternally.

And the Apostles "cast out many devils, and anointed with oil many that were sick, and healed them."

Valentine: Why did they anoint the sick with oil?

Grandma: It was oil which they had blessed in the name of Jesus. No doubt this was an image of Extreme Unction. Oil represents the unction and healing of the Holy Ghost.

Mary Theresa: What is Extreme Unction?

Grandma: It is a sacrament instituted by our Lord, for the dying, to give grace to those about to die, and to remit the sins they have committed.

Valentine: What is a sacrament?

Grandma: A sacrament is an outward sign instituted by Christ, to give grace, to scantify us in all the most important events of our life.

Valentine: What important events for instance?

Grandma: First: At our birth we are regenerated by *Baptism.*

Second: When we reach the age of reason we are sanctified and strengthened by *Confirmation.*

Third: As we grow older our souls are nourished and made to live in Christ by *Holy Communion.*

Fourth: When we have sinned we are forgiven and reconciled by *confession,* or, as it is called, the sacrament of *Penance.*

Fifth: Extreme Unction strengthens us and prepares us when we are about to die.

Sixth: Holy Orders is the sacrament in which the powers of the priesthood are conferred.

Seventh: Matrimony unites man and woman in indissoluble wedlock, and gives to that union the special blessing of God

The first five sacraments are for all and every one. The last two, Holy Orders and Matrimony, for those only who choose as a state of life the priesthood or the state of marriage.

CHAPTER XL.

BEHEADING OF JOHN THE BAPTIST.

Grandma: To-day, my children, I shall have to relate to you an incident that will shock and scandalize you. I shall have to tell you of the cruelty of Herod, the King.

Louis: The King Herod who murdered the little innocent babies when Jesus was born?

Grandma: No; this Herod had long since died and been succeeded by Archelaus, whom you recall reigned in his stead when Joseph brought back the Child Jesus from Egypt.

Archelaus reigned only one year, and in turn was succeeded by his wicked brother, Herod the Second. Some time before the incident I am about to relate, Herod ordered John the Baptist to be bound and cast into prison.

Jack: How dreadful! Why did Herod treat John the Baptist so cruelly?

Grandma: Herodias, the sister-in-law of Herod, had induced him to imprison John, whom she hated.

Louis: Why did Herodias hate John?

Grandma: John the Baptist, fearing no man, had publicly warned the King that the law forbade him to marry Herodias, his sister-in-law, while Philip, the husband of Herodias, still lived. However, Herodias, full of ambition—

Henry: What is ambition?

Grandma: To be ambitious is to love power and riches and honors. It is to desire to be more and to have more than one already possesses.

Herodias was ambitious to be made Queen, and St. John rightly and fearlessly prevented it. She sought means, therefore, to have the Baptist put to death. That he was bound and imprisoned did not satisfy her wicked desires. One day King Herod gave a great feast. It was his birthday, and he celebrated it with great pomp. To this feast, he invited all the great men of the court and their wives and the officers of his army.

The daughter of Herodias was among the invited guests, and to entertain the company she danced. She danced so well that Herod and his guests were delighted; and Herod, wishing to reward her, called her and said: "Ask of me what thou wilt, and I will will give it thee." And he swore that he would give her whatsoever she would ask, even though she asked for half of his kingdom.

The young woman consulted with her mother what she should ask the King, and Herodias, seizing this opportunity to obtain what she wished of Herod, bid her daughter ask for the head of John the Baptist.

The young woman, who was cruel and wicked as was her mother, returned to the banquet hall where they all sat at table, and said to the King: "Give me here in a dish the head of John the Baptist." This horrible request struck the King with sadness.

Though his conscience reproached him, he had promised before them all to give her what she asked, and he was ashamed to refuse her request. He ordered, therefore, one of his soldiers to behead John the Baptist in his prison. "And his head was brought in a dish; and it was given to the damsel, and she brought it to her mother."

The disciples of John, hearing of this, came and took his body and laid it in a tomb. Tradition tells us that later the head of the Baptist was found where it had been thrown, and that it was buried in the tomb where his body had long been interred.

Paul: What is a tradition?

Grandma: A tradition is the account of some event which happened in time past, which was not written down, but was told by word of mouth. An incident, for example, is witnessed by a number of people, and they tell their neighbors what they have seen and heard, and these friends tell their children, who, as they grow older, relate what was told them in their childhood; and so a truth comes down to us through the centuries.

CHAPTER XLI.

THE FEEDING OF THE MULTITUDE IN THE DESERT.

Grandma: The Apostles whom our Lord had sent out to teach the people, returned to give him an account of their labors. "Come apart into a desert place and rest a little," Christ said to them, "for there were so many coming and going that they had not so much as time to eat."

And entering one of the barks which lay anchored nearby, they crossed the sea of Tiberias, to a desert place beyond the lake. When the multitude saw Jesus set sail to cross the lake, the news of his going spread far and wide, and from the little towns and villages round about the people flocked to the opposite side of the lake to meet our Lord as he landed.

When Christ stepped from the bark with his disciples there they found the multitude eagerly awaiting his coming. Jesus took pity on this crowd, eager to hear his word, for they were as sheep without a shepherd, and forgetting his fatigue, he spoke to them for a long time of the kingdom of God.

It began to grow late and the disciples said to Christ: "Send away the multitude, that going into the towns and villages round about they may lodge and get victuals, for we are here in a desert place."

"But he said to them: Give you them to eat." Philip answering said to our Lord: "A hundred pennyworth of bread is not sufficient for them, that every one may take a little." And Jesus said to his disciples: "How many loaves have you? go and see." Andrew, Simon Peter's brother, returned, saying: "There is a boy here that hath five barley loaves and two fishes, but what is that among so many?" And Jesus ordered his disciples to make the people sit in groups on the green grass. The multitude numbered five thousand men alone, with many women and children.

Christ then took in his hands the five loaves and the two fishes and "looking up to heaven he blessed and broke the loaves and gave them to his disciples" to distribute among the people, "and the two fishes he divided among them all." And the Apostles distributed the loaves and fishes "and they all did eat and had their fill."

Jack: How was that possible?

Grandma: This was not only possible but easy for our Lord to accomplish. You know he was God, the Creator of all things. He multiplied and increased the bread and fishes, as the Apostles distributed them, just as he created the fishes that swim in the sea. When all had been satisfied, the disciples "took up the leavings, twelve full baskets of fragments." The people seeing this miracle said to one another: "This is of a truth the prophet that is to come into the world."

And Jesus sent his disciples across the lake in the boat to await his coming, "and having dismissed the multitude he went up to the mountain to pray."

CHAPTER XLII.

CHRIST WALKS UPON THE WATER.

Grandma: Our Lord, having dismissed the multitude, went up alone to the mountain to pray.

Madeleine: Grandma, one thing which surprises me is that our Lord prayed so frequently. Why did he pray? To whom did he pray, since he was God and equal to his Father?

Grandma: As Christ was true man as well as true God, Christ could pray to his Father. He prayed, first, to give us the example of prayer. Secondly, he prayed to adore God his Father, to thank him, to supplicate him, to beg of him forgiveness and mercy in the name of all mankind.

As I was saying, Christ withdrew to pray, while his disciples sailed towards Capernaum, there to await his coming. In the meantime a great storm arose and their bark was tossed by the waves. All night they rowed, but they could make no headway. Jesus, seeing his disciples struggling with wind and waves—

Valentine: How could Jesus see them from the mountain where he was praying?

Grandma: With the power which belongs to God who sees all things, Christ saw the ship out on the lake of Tiberius. Seeing their danger he went to their help, walking on the water. The disciples seeing Jesus coming to them on the water, thought they saw an apparition, and they were frightened. But immediately he spoke to them saying: "Be of good heart, it is I, fear not."

Peter answered saying: "Lord, if it be thou, bid me come to thee upon the waters." "Come," said Jesus, and Peter getting out of the boat walked on the water to go to his master. But suddenly, the wind blowing with greater violence, Peter was frightened and he began to sink and he cried out: "Lord, save me." "And immediately Jesus, stretching forth his hand, took hold of him and said to him: O thou of little faith, why didst thou doubt?"

Henry: I can understand how frightened St. Peter was. I would have been frightened too in his place.

Grandma: And it would have been wrong of you, as it was of St. Peter. He began to sink only when he began to be afraid. Doubting the power of Christ to hold him on the surface of the water, he began to fear and he sank. If Peter had more faith, he would have known he was safe. He doubted, and he had witnessed so many miracles showing the power of Christ. Only a few days before he had seen five barley loaves and two fishes multiplied to feed five thousand people! Christ punished his want of faith, and at the same time increased his faith, by permitting him to sink. Fortunately he called on Christ at once to save him.

Like St. Peter, when we feel inclined to sin, near to sinking under temptation, we should call on Jesus for help. He will always come to our aid, as he did to St. Peter's. He held out his hand and helped him into the boat, and the storm ceased immediately.

The disciples were amazed at this miracle. They were so blind of heart, these disciples! They understood so faintly who our Lord was. The miracle of the loaves and fishes had not opened their eyes. But after having seen him walk on the waters and quiet the tempest, they drew near to Jesus and adored him saying: "Indeed, thou art the Son of God."

Having crossed the lake, they landed in the country of Genesareth.

No sooner had Christ landed, than the good news spread far and wide. The people flocked to him, from the villages and hamlets nearby, and they brought to him their sick and maimed, "and besought him that they might touch but the hem of his garment; and as many as touched him were made whole."

CHAPTER XLIII.

THE PROMISE OF THE EUCHARIST.

Grandma: The next day the multitude, whom Jesus had left at Tiberius, set out to seek him, and not finding him, they crossed over the Sea of Tiberius in their barks to Capernaum. Having found Christ on the opposite shore, they said to him in surprise: "Master, when camest thou hither?"

Jesus read their hearts and knew that they sought him with such eagerness, not because of the truths he taught them, but because of the bread with which he had fed them in the wilderness. Therefore, without replying to their question, he told them that this life was not the eternal life, that the bread with which he had fed them in the desert was not the bread of eternal life which he would give them. "They said therefore to him: Lord give us always this bread." And Jesus said to them: "I am the living bread which came down from heaven." In beautiful words, which you will all read when you are as old as Camille and Elizabeth, Christ told them that the bread of eternal life of which he spoke was himself—his own flesh and blood, with which he would feed all men. And that those who would not eat of this bread, would not have eternal life. That they would not live in him, nor he in them.

Henry: Grandma, I don't understand at all. How can we eat our Lord and how can he give himself to all men as food?

Grandma: Our Lord left us his body to be our food in the Blessed Sacrament of the Eucharist. In this Sacrament he continues for us the miracle of the multiplication of the loaves. Christ Jesus hides himself under the appearance of the bread given in Communion. Those who receive Communion receive truly and really the body and blood of Christ, hidden under the appearance of the Sacred Host and multiplied an infinite number of times, that all who wish may receive him.

Though he is hidden thus under the appearance of bread, he is truly present. Hence we call the host "the bread of life." And he said to the Jews: "I am the living bread which came down from heaven. If any man eat of this bread he shall live forever; and the bread that I will give is my flesh, for the life of the world. . . . Amen, amen I say unto you; except you eat the flesh of the Son of Man, and drink his blood, you shall not have life in you. He that eateth my flesh, and drinketh my blood, hath everlasting life; and I will raise him up on the last day. For my flesh is meat indeed; and my blood is drink indeed. . . . This is the bread which came down from heaven. . . . He that eateth this bread shall live forever."

The Jews and even the disciples who heard Jesus did not understand him. They thought this blessed promise strange and impossible.

Jesus, who could read their hardened hearts, read these thoughts and continued speaking to them of the Eucharist; but many left him and would no longer be his disciples, because they would not believe.

Then Jesus, saddened at their hardness of heart, turned to the twelve disciples who stood around him and said to them: "Will you also go away? And Simon Peter answered him: Lord to whom shall we go? Thou hast the words of eternal life. And we have believed and have known that thou art the Christ, the Son of God."

Jesus looked at him lovingly and said: "Have I not chosen you twelve; and one of you is a devil?"

Our Lord here referred to Judas, who was to betray him, and who was one of the twelve whom he had chosen as his special friends.

From that time Jesus remained in Galilee, avoiding the country of Judea, because the Jews sought to put him to death, and the hour of his sacrifice had not yet come.

He preached in the country round about, and in the synagogues. In his many discourses, which we read in the Gospels, Christ Jesus sought to impress on all who heard him that it was not only the observing of the Law which pleased God, but the good dispositions of the heart—humility, patience, purity, charity. He explained that it would avail them nothing to have fasted and offered up sacrifices, if in their hearts they entertained evil thoughts. For, Christ said to them: "Not that which goeth into the mouth defileth a man; but that which cometh out of a man, this defileth a man."

Little Louis: What does that mean, defileth?

Grandma: To defile means to soil. Our souls are defiled by sin only. Our Lord meant what comes out of man's heart alone can stain or hurt his soul.

CHAPTER XLIV.

THE CANAANITISH WOMAN.

Grandma: One day, as Christ was passing on the road near Tyre and Sidon—

Paul: What were Tyre and Sidon?

Grandma: These were two wealthy towns of Phoenicia in Syria.   From out of the city of Tyre there came to Jesus a Canaanitish woman—

Paul: What does Canaanitish mean?

Grandma: It means of the tribe of Canaan. These people dwelt in Syria.   They were idolaters. That is to say, they worshipped false gods and images of false gods which they had made according to their fancy.   This woman had heard of the miracles of Jesus, and she came to him crying out and saying: "Have mercy on me, O Lord, thou Son of David; my daughter is grievously troubled by a devil."

To this appeal Jesus answered not a word, and seemed unmindful of her petition.   The woman continued to cry out, asking help for her daughter; and the disciples, wearied by her importunity, begged our Lord to heed her cry, saying: "Send her away, for she keeps crying after us."

And Jesus answering said: "I was not sent but to the sheep that are lost of the house of Israel."

Mary Theresa: What did that mean? To what sheep had he been sent?

Grandma: Our Lord spoke of the people of Israel as the sheep to whom he had been sent. This Jewish people you know, were his chosen people, from whom was born the Blessed Virgin Mary, the mother of Christ, the Messias who was to save the world. Therefore this, his chosen people, were to hear his word before all the other nations of the world. Another motive which induced our Lord to refuse to answer the supplications of this Canaanitish woman was that Christ wanted to teach us to persevere in prayer and not be discouraged, but to beg with oft-repeated supplications for what we need.

Undaunted by his silence, the woman drew nearer and adored him, saying "Lord, help me." Who answering said: "It is not good to take the bread of the children, and to cast it to the dogs."

Valentine: The poor woman was not asking for bread, but for her daughter's cure. I don't understand that.

Grandma: Our Lord wished to prove her humility. He expresses in these words that the Jews are his children, his favored people, and that to them is reserved the bread of his miracles. And, moreover, that the race of Canaan are idolaters, and he speaks of them as of a race of dogs, unworthy to receive this bread.

Jane: It is strange to me that our Lord, who was so good, should be so severe to this woman.

Grandma: Our Lord was goodness itself, and could not be severe.   He was not severe to this poor woman, nor is he severe to us when he sends us illness and afflictions.   He allows these trials only to increase our merit; to be able to reward our patience and perseverance and resignation, as you will see in the case of this poor woman.   Very humbly she answered our Lord: "Yea, Lord; for the whelps also eat of the crumbs that fall from the table of their masters."

Looking at her with compassion, Jesus said to her: "O woman great is thy faith; be it done to thee as thou wilt."

And the woman, returning to her home, found her daughter cured.

We read of no other miracles performed in this country.   Jesus left this pagan land, and crossing Sidon again reached the Sea of Galilee.

CHAPTER XLV.

CURE OF THE DEAF AND DUMB MAN.

Grandma: When Christ reached the coast of the Sea of Galilee a man deaf and dumb was brought to him to be cured.

Jesus taking him aside put his fingers in his ears, and wetting his fingers with saliva, touched his tongue, then he raised his eyes to heaven, he sighed, and said: "Ephpheta, which means, be thou opened. And immediately his ears were opened, the string of his tongue was loosed, and the dumb man spake distinctly." And all who witnessed this miracle were in amazement, and they said: "He hath done all things well: he hath made both the deaf to hear and the dumb to speak."

Elizabeth: Why did our Lord do so many and such various things to cure this man? In other cures he merely spoke and they were healed; but to cure this man he puts his fingers in the poor man's ears, saliva on his tongue, he raises up his eyes, he sighs, and says: "Be thou opened" before the man is cured.

Grandma: This cure is a type or picture given for our instruction of the conversion of sinners. This

man, we are told, was *brought* to Jesus. Evidently
he does not come to Christ of his own accord, and
even then our Lord has to take him by the hand
and draw him to himself aside from the crowd.
This indicates the unwillingness of the sinner to be
converted. Then our Lord himself has to touch
the heart of the sinner by his grace. Even that is
not enough, and Jesus prays to his Father, and lastly,
it is only when Christ commands that his eyes are
opened. The sinner at last sees and acknowledges
his sins, and they are forgiven, by reason of his
repentance and God's great mercy.

CHAPTER XLVI.

JESUS FEEDS THE MULTITUDE.

Grandma: After this miracle, Jesus withdrew to the mountains near the lake. There the multitude found him. They came in great numbers, "bringing with them the dumb, the blind, the maimed, and many others, and they cast them down at his feet and he healed them." "So that the multitude marveled, seeing the dumb speak, the lame walk, the blind see, and they glorified the God of Israel."

"And Jesus called together his disciples, and said: I have compassion on the multitude, because they have been with me now three days and have not what to eat, and I will not send them away fasting, lest they faint in the way." And the disciples, no doubt forgetting how he had miraculously fed the five thousand in the wilderness, asked him: "Whence, then, can any one fill them with bread here in the desert? And he asked them: How many loaves have you? But they said: Seven and a few little fishes."

And a second time Jesus multiplied the bread and fishes to feed this multitude of hungry people, who had come to hear his word and to be healed. He blessed the bread and the fishes and gave them to his disciples and they distributed them, and by his almighty power there was enough for all, and seven baskets full left over.

"And having dismissed the multitude, he went up into a boat and came into the coasts of Magedan."

Louis: Where was the country of Magedan?

Grandma: Between Genesareth and Corozain, and very near the Sea of Galilee.

CHAPTER XLVII.

THE CURE OF THE BLIND MAN.

Grandma: Jesus and his disciples crossed the Sea of Galilee to Bethsaida, a town on the seacoast. Here they brought to him a blind man, beseeching Christ to cure him. Jesus took him by the hand and led him aside, and putting spittle on his eyes asked him if he saw anything. The blind man looking up answered: "I see men as it were trees walking." Jesus again laid his blessed hands on the poor, half-opened eyes, and the blind man "began to see and was restored, so that he saw all things clearly," and Jesus sent him back to his house, cured.

Louis: This miracle reminds me of the deaf and dumb man. Our Lord had so much trouble curing him also.

Grandma: Yes; in this instance, also, we see the picture of a converted sinner. The soul must leave bad habits and evil acquaintances, and go aside with Jesus, if it will be cured. In the beginning of his conversion, the sinner sees only indistinctly, as did the blind man when Jesus first touched his eyes. However, he begins to see the world as it is and all things in a better light; but it is only after his soul is washed by sacramental grace that his eyes are opened. This means, of course, the eyes of his soul. He then sees his sins and sees the difference between good and evil, and his soul is cured.

BOOK FOURTH

Third Year of the Ministry of Jesus

CHAPTER XLVIII.

CHRIST ESTABLISHES PETER HEAD OF HIS CHURCH.

Grandma: Jesus left Bethsaida in the company of his disciples to visit the neighboring villages of Judea, situated near the mouth of the Jordan. And on the way Jesus put this question to his disciples: "Whom do men say that I am?" And they anwered: "Some say John the Baptist; and some say Elias; and others say that one of the former prophets is risen again."

Jesus said to them: "But whom do you say that I am?"

"Simon Peter answered and said: Thou art Christ, the Son of the living God."

"And Jesus answering said to him: Blessed art thou, Simon, son of John, because flesh and blood hath not revealed it to thee, but my Father who is in heaven. And I say to thee, that thou art Peter; and upon this rock I will build my Church, and the gates of hell shall not prevail against it. And I will give to thee the keys of the kingdom of heaven. And whatsoever thou shalt bind upon earth, it shall be bound also in heaven; and whatsoever thou shalt loose on earth, it shall be loosed also in heaven."

Louis. What does "flesh and blood" mean? How can flesh and blood reveal anything?

Grandma: By "flesh and blood" our Lord means our human intelligence, which would not have been capable of showing St. Peter that Christ was the Son of God unless the grace of God had come to his aid.

Henrietta: And what does our Lord mean when he says that on St. Peter he will build his Church?

Grandma: When we plan to build a house, we begin by laying a foundation stone, a first stone, on which all the other stones will be laid for the erection of the building. Likewise, when our Lord planned his Church, he established St. Peter as the corner stone. It was on this foundation stone, Peter, who was the first Pontiff, that the Church of Christ was erected. From this beginning it was built up and is still being erected, composed of the faithful who form the Church. These faithful followers of Christ are guided and directed by the Sovereign Pontiff, the Holy Father, who is the successor of St. Peter. Each one of us is as a stone in this edifice.

Valentine: What means "the gates of hell shall not prevail against it"?

Grandma: The gates of hell signify the powers of hell. These are the spirits of evil, the heretics, the unbelievers, who attack the Church of Christ, and endeavor to overthrow it. Our Lord promised that they would not succeed, because he had established it on a strong foundation, St. Peter, and his successors, the Bishops of Rome.

The teachings of the Holy Father, who is the Bishop of Rome, and his decisions guide the Church of Christ to-day. And the faithful yielding him all obedience, strong in their faith, will never be overthrown.

Louis: What keys did our Lord give St. Peter?

Grandma: This also is what we call a figure of speech; that is to say, it holds a meaning, a lesson, which I shall give you.

As a householder gives his overseer all the keys which lock up the treasures of his house, Christ gives to Peter, whom he has just established Head of the Church, power to give out or withhold the treasures of that Church.

All that Peter will bind, that is, condemn, will be bound and condemned by our Lord in heaven; all that he will approve and forgive, will be approved and forgiven in heaven.

The Pope, as the representative of Christ, is the visible Head of the Church. In matters of the Christian religion, then, every one owes him, as they owe Christ, obedience; and this is true even of kings, emperors, and bishops.

CHAPTER XLIX.

CHRIST PREDICTS HIS DEATH AND RESURRECTION.

Grandma: Then, still speaking to his disciples, our Lord predicted his death. He told them he would have to go to Jerusalem to suffer, and that the scribes and princes and high priests would put him to death; but that on the third day he would rise again from the dead.

Peter, taking our Lord aside, "began to rebuke him saying: Lord, be it far from thee, this shall not be unto thee." But Jesus, turning to Peter, said to him: "Go behind me, Satan, thou art a scandal unto me; because thou savorest not the things that are of God, but the things that are of men."

Henrietta: Poor St. Peter, why does our Lord rebuke him so severely? It does not seem to me he said anything wrong.

Grandma: Our Lord shows Peter his displeasure in these strong words, to show him how guilty he was to wish to oppose his will to the will of God. He teaches Peter and the other disciples that, however repugnant and distasteful may be the duties, trials and sorrows of this life, we must accept them with love and joy, because they are sent by God.

We must not rebel against them, but we must perform these duties and bear these hardships willingly.

Around the little group of Apostles the people began to gather, and our Lord addressing them all added "If any man will come after me, let him deny himself, and take up his cross, and follow me."

Valentine: What did Christ mean by that?

Grandma: This means that all of us who wish to become good Christians and enter into the kingdom of God, must deny ourselves, that is, overcome ourselves, conquer our faults and failings. We must take up our cross, which means we must bear without murmuring all the sorrows and sufferings which may come to us. It means we must impose on ourselves privations for the love of God.

Valentine: What privations, Grandma?

Grandma: The privation of what may be a pleasure to us, if it is bad for our souls. For example, the idle man will work, though inclined to be indolent; the glutton will moderate his appetite; the vain man will give up the desire to please and to be praised, the liar will strive not to alter the truth; those given to anger will endeavor to be gentle and patient, though it cost them an effort. All this you see includes privations, the denying of our own will.

When we thus deny ourselves we follow in the footsteps of Christ, our Lord, and he will lead us to his heavenly kingdom.

And Christ added: "For whosoever will save his life, shall lose it; and whosoever shall lose his life for my sake, shall find it; for what shall it profit a man if he gain the whole world, and suffer the loss of his soul?"

Henry: Must we not try to save our life if we are in danger?

Grandma: Yes; we can and must save our life and preserve our life, provided thereby we do not deny our Lord. Christ here speaks of those who prefer death to denying Christ by sin. These he tells us will find eternal life in heaven. On the other hand, they who, for the sake of life on earth, deny Christ, will be lost eternally.

What good, indeed, will it do us if, in order to be happy in this world for a few years, we should lose our soul and be unhappy for all eternity.

CHAPTER L.

THE TRANSFIGURATION OF OUR LORD.

Grandma: About eight days after this instruction to his disciples Christ, taking with him Peter and James and John, ascended a steep mountain to pray, undisturbed.

And while our Lord Jesus prayed "his face did shine as the sun, and his garments became white as snow."

Peter and the other two Apostles, weary with the day's journeyings, had fallen asleep, but the bright light, which surrounded Christ aroused them; and they awoke to find their Master resplendent with a heavenly glory and conversing with two men, whom they saw were Moses and Elias. Together they were speaking with our Lord of his death, which would take place in Jerusalem. Peter bewildered and amazed, cried out: "Master, it is good for us to be here, let us make three tabernacles, one for thee one for Moses, one for Elias!"

While Peter was still speaking a bright cloud enveloped Jesus and Moses and Elias, and from this mist the Apostles heard a voice saying: "This is my beloved Son; here ye him." Filled with fear at this glorious vision, the Apostles fell prostrate on the ground, and Jesus drawing near touched them saying: "Arise, and fear not."

"And they, lifting up their eyes, saw no one, but only Jesus. And as they came down from the mountain Jesus charged them, saying: Tell the vision to no man, till the Son of Man be risen from the dead." And the Apostles obeyed our Lord, but they questioned among themselves what meant, "when he shall be risen from the dead?"

Jack: What, they did not yet understand what our Lord had told them of his death and resurrection?

Grandma: Their minds were still unopened to the truth. It was needful that Christ should die and rise again, and that the light of the Holy Ghost should come upon his Apostles before they should be strong in their faith. Not until then did they understand fully who Christ was, and why he had come into this world, why he had died, and how he had proved his divinity by his resurrection.

Henry: And yet we understand all that.

Grandma: Yes; we understand because of the grace of Baptism, which implants in our souls the seed of faith, and because of the teachings of the Church of Christ.

CHAPTER LI.

THE HEALING OF THE BOY POSSESSED OF THE DEVIL.

Grandma: The following day, as Jesus came down from the mountain with his three Apostles, he saw a crowd gathered around the disciples whom he had left at the foot of the mount to await his return. And, as he drew near, a man from the crowd cried out: "Master, I beseech thee, look upon my son, because he is my only one. And, lo! a spirit seizeth him and he suddenly crieth out, and he throweth him down and teareth him, so that he foameth and gnasheth with the teeth; and I spoke to thy disciples to cast him out, and they were not able." Jesus said: "Bring hither thy son." And as the child drew near to Jesus, "the devil threw him down upon the ground." And Jesus asked the father: "How long time is it since this hath happened unto him?" And the father answered: "From this infancy. And oftentimes hath he (the evil spirit) cast him into the fire and into water to destroy him. But if thou canst do anything, help us, having compassion on us. Jesus said to him: If thou canst believe, all things are possible to him that believeth. And immediately the father of the boy cried out, with tears said   I do believe, Lord, help thou my unbelief." And Jesus threatened the unclean spirit, saying: "Deaf and dumb spirit I command thee, go out of him, and enter not any more into him."

And crying out, the evil spirit left the child, who lay on the ground as if dead.

"But Jesus, taking him by the hand, lifted him up and he rose," and Jesus gave him to his father restored to health.

Jane: Why could not the disciples cure this child?

Grandma: Because they had not sufficient faith in the power Christ Jesus had given them.

Henry: And why does our Lord ask the father to believe before he cures the child? It would not have been the child's fault if his father had not believed.

Grandma: It was the father who asked the cure of his son. It was to the father our Lord granted the cure. And the father had to deserve it by his faith in the power of Christ, whose aid he sought.

Elizabeth: Why does our Lord say: "Thou deaf and dumb spirit?"

Grandma: Because the evil spirit had made the poor boy deaf and dumb.

Elizabeth: Are there persons to-day possessed of the devil?

Grandma: In Christian countries, since the coming of Christ, it is very rare. However, it is not unknown in pagan countries. In China, for instance, there are such cases.

Elizabeth: And how are they cured, these poor people?

Grandma: They are exorcised; that is to say, that the priest sprinkles them with holy water, says certain prayers over them and for them, and often obtains their deliverance from the power of the evil one.

Camille: A few days ago, when I was visiting with mother, I heard some one say that there was no such thing as possession by the devil; that persons who seemed so afflicted were only ill.

Grandma: Those who speak thus, either do not reflect, or have not sufficient faith. If we believe in the Bible, we must necessarily believe in the devil and the possibility of his taking possession of us. Unfortunately, cases of possession do exist, and we can't disbelieve them. But if we live good, pure, Christian lives, we are under the protection of our Lord, who is all-powerful, and consequently we are safe from the power of Satan.

While the people wondered among themselves at this miracle, our Lord entered the house. His disciples asked him: "Why could we not cast out the devil?" And Jesus answered them: "Because of your unbelief. For, amen, I say to you, if ye have faith as a grain of mustard seed, you shall say to this mountain: Remove from hence, and it shall remove, and nothing will be impossible to you.

Leaving the neighborhood of Mount Tabor, Jesus and his disciples took the road to Capernaum. On the way Jesus said to them: "The Son of Man shall be betrayed into the hands of men, and they shall kill him; and after that he is killed, he shall rise again the third day."

But the disciples did not understand these words, though they were very clear and easy to comprehend.

CHAPTER LII.

JESUS PAYS THE TRIBUTE MONEY.

Grandma: Having reached Capernaum, the collector of taxes drew near to St. Peter and said to him. "Doth not your Master pay the two didrachma for the tribute?"

Paul: What was the tribute?

Grandma: The tribute is a certain sum of money which all conquered countries must pay every year to their conquerors. The Jews, therefore, owed tribute to the Romans since the conquest of Judea by Rome.

Little Louis: What is the didrachma?

Grandma: A didrachma is a small piece of money worth about ten cents of our money.

"Yes;" Peter replied, "he pays it." And going into the house, Peter spoke to our Lord of the demand of the tax gatherer. Jesus explained to St. Peter that, being king of earth and heaven, he did not owe this tribute; but, added Jesus, "that we may not scandalize them go to the sea, and cast in a hook; and that fish which shall first come up, take; and when thou hast opened its mouth, thou shalt find a stater; take that, and give it to them for thee and for me."

Henrietta: What is a stater?

Grandma: A stater is a piece of money worth about four didrachmas, that would be forty cents of our money. And so our Lord paid the tribute for himself and St. Peter, in obedience to the law.

CHAPTER LIII.

DISPUTE AMONG THE DISCIPLES.

Grandma: When they had re-entered the house, Jesus asked his disciples: "What were you discussing on the road?" The disciples quite abashed did not reply, "for on the way they had disputed among themselves, which of them should be greatest!" And Christ seating himself drew a little child to him, and held the little one in his embrace, and to his disciples he said: "If any man desire to be first, he shall be the last of all, and the servant of all."

Louis: Why should such a man be the last of all?

Grandma: This expression, the last of all, means here the most humble. Our Lord loves the humble-minded; he abhors the proud. When we are the least in our own esteem; when we realize our sinfulness, and how little we deserve reward, then our soul is prepared to receive the graces of God. Then we are near to sanctity and to the bliss of heaven.

And after embracing the little child, he set him in the midst of them and said to them: "Amen I say to you, unless you be converted, and become as little children, you shall not enter into the kingdom of heaven. Whosoever, therefore, shall humble himself as this little child, he is the greater in the kingdom of heaven. And he that shall receive one such little child in my name, receiveth me. But he that shall scandalize one of these little ones that believe in me, it were better for him that a millstone should be hanged about his neck, and that he should be drowned in the depth of the sea."

Henrietta: It must be a terrible thing then to scandalize a child.

Grandma: You see how terrible our Lord thinks it is, since he tells his disciples it were better for the culprit to be drowned in the depths of the sea. It is, indeed, dreadfully wicked to scandalize a little child; to teach him evil ways; to lessen his faith; to kill the life of his soul; those souls of little children, so innocent and pure.

When you grow up, my little children, love the little ones as our Lord loved them. Be good and gentle to them; instruct them; give them good advice and good example; comfort them in their little difficulties. Never take advantage of your greater strength over those that are without means of defence, but sweeten their lives and teach them gentleness and love. Train their young hearts to the love of God. Imitate our Lord, love them, embrace them, and remember these words of Christ: "He that shall receive a little child in my name receiveth me."

Camille: Grandma, is that the reason you love little children so much?

Grandma: Yes, little one; for that reason, and also because I naturally love little children.

Our Lord continued teaching his disciples, saying to them: "And if thy hand scandalize thee, cut it off—".

Henrietta: Oh, my! this is the second time our Lord says this!

Grandma, continuing: "It is better for thee to enter into life maimed than having two hands to go into hell. And if thy foot scandalize thee, cut it off. It is better for thee to enter lame into life everlasting, than having two feet to be cast into the hell of unquenchable fire, where the fire is not extinguished. And if thy eye scandalize thee pluck it out. It is better for thee with one eye to enter into the kingdom of God than, having two eyes, to be cast into the hell of fire."

Henrietta: Grandma, it is really impossible to obey our Lord's command. I, for one, won't cut off my hands and feet and pluck out my eyes.

Grandma: You have already forgotten what I told you only a few days ago, that our Lord speaks by means of comparisons, of figures of speech. He wants to teach us that we must be ready to sacrifice even the most necessary, even the most innocent things, rather than commit a sin. As a figure of speech, you will cut off your hands and your feet by preventing them, through your will, to do evil. Twice does our Lord repeat this precept, in order to show us how necessary such a determination is to us.

Our Lord ended this instruction by telling his disciples that when two or three persons were gathered together to pray, their request would be answered by their Father in heaven; for, said Jesus: "Where there are two or three gathered together in my name, there I am in the midst of them."

CHAPTER LIV.

PARABLE OF THE KING AND HIS SERVANTS.

Grandma: Peter, who had listened to this beautiful discourse, drew near to Jesus and said: "Lord how often shall my brother offend against me, and I forgive him? till seven times?"

Jesus answered: "I say not to thee, till seven times; but till seventy times seven times."

Henry: Why does our Lord mention this special number?

Grandma: This large number signified that we must forgive always, and always without growing weary

And, continued our Lord: "Therefore is the kingdom of heaven likened to a king, who would take an account of his servants. And when he had begun to take the account, one was brought to him that owed him ten thousand talents."

Mary Theresa: What is a talent?

Grandma: A talent was a piece of money used by the Hebrews, and worth about one thousand nine hundred dollars of our money. In mentioning ten thousand talents, our Lord wishes to indicate a very large sum.

"And as the servant had not wherewith to pay it, his lord commanded that he should be sold, and his wife and children and all that he had, and payment to be made."

Valentine: What a wicked king!

Grandma: Wait and you will hear the end of this parable: "But that servant falling down, besought him, saying: Have patience with me, and I will pay thee all. And the lord of that servant, being moved with pity, let him go and forgave him his debt. But when that servant had gone out, he found one of his fellow-servants that owed him a hundred pence."

Paul: What is a pence?

Grandma: A pence is a small piece of Roman money, worth about eighteen cents.

The servant having met his fellow-servant, who owed him one hundred pence, "throttled him, saying: Pay what thou owest. And his fellow-servant, falling down, besought him, saying: Have patience with me, and I will pay thee all. And he would not; but went and cast him into prison, till he paid his debt. Now his fellow-servants, seeing what was done, were very much grieved, and they came and told their lord all that was done. Then his lord called him, and said to him: Thou wicked servant, I forgave thee all thy debt, because thou besoughtest me. Shouldst not thou then have had compassion also on thy fellow-servant, even as

I had compassion on thee. And his lord, being angry, delivered him to the torturers until he paid all his debt. So, also, shall my heavenly father do to you, if you forgive not every one his brother from your hearts."

Louis: However, Grandma, if we owe money we have to pay it. Would it not be dishonest not to pay back what we borrow?

Grandma: Our Lord in this parable uses money as an example. He means the forgiveness of injuries, the pardon of offences. The wicked servant owed the king a large sum, that is to say he had greatly offended his king, as we may have committed many offences against God. His master determines to punish him by imprisonment for those things of which he is guilty. The servant, frightened, begs pardon of his lord, implores his mercy, promises to atone by good conduct in the future. The master is good; he is moved to pity, and he forgives his servant. Though not in money, it is really a debt the master remits, or forgives. The wicked servant meets a man who has only slightly offended him. He lays hold of him and casts him into prison. This means, he returns him evil for evil, does him injury, and this in spite of the supplications of his enemy, who promises to be his friend in the future, thus to repay or atone for the wrong he has done him. Then the king, seeing that the wicked servant had taken no heed of the example of forgiveness of injuries which he had but now given him, withdrew his forgiveness.

This parable shows us plainly that we should be charitable and forgive our enemies, if we wish the good God, our Divine Master, to forgive us our sins.

CHAPTER LV.

THE SAMARITANS REFUSE TO RECEIVE JESUS.

Grandma: Our Lord, with his Apostles, took the road to Jerusalem. On the way they came to a Samaritan village, and Christ sent his disciples ahead to prepare a lodging place for them.

But the inhabitants of Samaria hated the Jews, and would not receive them into their city. The disciples, James and John, returned to Jesus, saying: "Lord, wilt thou that we command fire to come down from heaven, and consume them? But Jesus rebuked them, saying: You know not of what spirit you are."

Mary Theresa: What did that mean, Grandma?

Grandma: Our Lord meant: you forget that ye should have the spirit of charity, which is the spirit of God, my spirit, I who am all meekness and all charity. Then our Lord added: "The Son of God came not to destroy souls, but to save." And they went further into another village, and as they journeyed a man drew near to our Lord saying: "I will follow thee whithersoever thou goest. Jesus said to him: The foxes have holes and the birds of the air have nests: but the Son of Man hath not where to lay his head."

Jane: Poor Jesus! he had not even a little house of his own.

Grandma: If Christ had willed it, he could have had all the wealth of the world; but he willed to spend all the days of his earthly life in poverty, destitute of all things, to give us an example of detachment from riches and the things of this world.

Therefore, to those who felt drawn to follow him, but hesitated because the affairs of this world detained them, our Lord said: "No man putting his hand to the plow, and looking back, is fit for the kingdom of God."

Valentine: What does that mean?

Grandma: This means that he is a poor servant who, after having begun to work for God and to serve him, casts a backward glance of regret on the friends and pleasures he has left. He will soon leave the plow, which means the life of mortification and of penance, and abandon God's service for the world.

CHAPTER LVI.

PARABLE OF THE GOOD SAMARITAN.

Grandma: One day a Doctor of the Law said to Jesus: "Master, what shall I do to obtain eternal life?" Jesus saw at a glance that this man questioned him not in order to learn, but hoping to induce our Lord to answer something that would displease the people. None the less Christ deigns to teach him; and replies by a question: "What is written in the law?" The lawyer answered: "Thou shalt love the Lord thy God with thy whole heart, and with thy whole soul, and with thy whole strength, and with all thy mind; and thy neighbor as thyself." And Jesus said to him: "Thou hast answered right; this do, and thou shalt live." But the lawyer, wishing to appear eager to understand the law, asked our Lord who was his neighbor? And Jesus replied: "A certain man went from Jerusalem to Jericho—"

Little Louis: Was Jericho very far away?

Grandma: Jericho was a city about ten miles from Jerusalem.

Well, this man going to Jericho "fell among robbers, who stripped him, and having wounded him went away, leaving him half dead. And it chanced a certain priest went down the same way; and seeing him, passed by. In like manner, also, a Levite, when he was near the place, saw him, and passed by. But a certain Samaritan, being on his journey, came near him, and seeing him was moved with compassion. And going up to him, bound up his wounds, pouring in oil and wine; and setting him upon his own beast, brought him to an inn and took care of him. And the next day he took out two pence, and give it to the host, and said: Take care of him; and whatsoever thou shalt spend over and above, I, at my return, will repay thee."

And our Lord asked the lawyer which of these three men had shown himself neighbor to the poor man? and he answered: "He that showed mercy to him. And Jesus said to him: Go, and do thou in like manner."

Henry: Grandma, why does our Lord give a parable in which he shows the priests and Levites as unkind to this poor man, and the Samaritan good to him? Yet, the priests were Jews, and his chosen people, were they not?

Grandma: Our Lord purposely tells this parable to humble the Levites and priests, who thought themselves superior to all other men, and who despised the Samaritans especially. He wished to teach that all men had a right to God's grace and favor, and that he had come to save all men.

CHAPTER LVII.

MARTHA AND MARY.

Grandma: Jesus, in his journey through Judea, stopped on the way at the village of Bethany. Here dwelt Lazarus, whom Jesus loved, and with him his two sisters, Martha and Mary. In their house our Lord stopped and accepted the hospitality they offered him.

While Martha busied herself with great concern to prepare the evening meal for our Lord, and all things needful to his comfort, Mary sat at our Lord's feet listening to his words. Martha said to Christ: "Lord, hast thou no care that my sister hath left me alone to serve? Speak to her, therefore, that she help me. And the Lord answering said to her: Martha, Martha, thou art careful, and art troubled about many things. But one thing is necessary. Mary hath chosen the best part, which shall not be taken away from her."

Louis: It seems to me Martha was right in complaining that Mary did not help her; for, after all, Martha was very busy because she wanted to give Jesus a good meal.

Grandma: And our Lord does not blame her. He only shows her that those things which fill her mind are of very little importance. He tells her only *one thing is necessary*.

Jack: And he don't tell her what that one thing is?

Grandma: Yes; he indicates plainly what it is; for he says: Mary has chosen the better part, which is to remain near him listening to his words and drawing profit from his teaching. And Christ adds, that he will not compel her to give up this happiness.

Jack: Then Martha had to do the work alone?

Grandma: It is likely Martha had servants to carry out her orders, for Lazarus was a rich man. Herein our Lord gives Martha, as well as ourselves, a lesson. He warns us against worrying and fretting over the things of this world to the extent of neglecting the things of God.

Jack: But some one had to prepare what our Lord needed.

Grandma: Yes; but not at the cost of neglecting our Lord himself. Here we see Martha leaving our Lord's company to prepare for him a good evening meal, for which our Lord cared very little.

Jane: That's true, she should have given her orders to the servants, and listened to our Lord, together with Mary.

Grandma: This reproach which Martha made to

Mary Magdalene, and to which our Lord replies so
clearly, is still made by people living in the world
to those who are living in convents. They judge
that the religious are leading useless lives.   But to
this reproach we have the reply of our Lord to Martha,
that they have chosen the better part, which shall
not be taken from them.

CHAPTER LVIII.

THE BARREN FIG TREE.

Grandma: One day our Lord gave the following parable to his disciples: "A certain man had a fig tree planted in his vineyard, and he came seeking fruit on it, and found none. And he said to the dresser of the vineyard: Behold, for these three years I come seeking fruit on this fig tree, and I find none. Cut it down, therefore; why cumbereth it the ground? But he, answering, said to him: Lord, let it alone this year also, until I dig about it, and dung it. And if happily it bear fruit; but if not, then after that thou shalt cut it down."

Valentine: What does this parable mean, Grandma?

Grandma: The fig tree, cultivated and carefully tended, is the figure of a soul encouraged and trained to bear fruit—the fruits of good deeds. The good God waits patiently, but seeing that this soul bears no fruit in spite of the care lavished upon it by the vine dresser, who represents the priests, he orders that it be cut down. This means abandoned, left to itself. But the priest intercedes for this soul,

and begs our Lord to wait, pleading that, with time
this soul may be converted and bear fruit for his
kingdom.   And the voice of the priest is heard.
God is good and consents to wait.

CHAPTER LIX.

THE CURE OF THE WOMAN BENT DOUBLE.

Grandma: One Sabbath day our Lord was teaching in the synagogue and "there was a woman who had a spirit of infirmity eighteen years; and she was bowed together, neither could she look upwards at all." Jesus seeing the poor woman so grievously afflicted, called her to him and said to her: "Woman, thou art delivered from thy infirmity. And he laid his hands upon her, and immediately she was made straight and glorified God."

And the ruler of the synagogue was angry that Jesus had healed on the Sabbath day and he said to the people: "Six days there are wherein you ought to work. In them, therefore, come and be healed; and not on the Sabbath day."

But Jesus replied: "Ye hypocrites, doth not every one of you, on the Sabbath day, loose his ox or his ass from the manger, and lead them to water? And ought not this daughter of Abraham, whom Satan hath bound, lo, these eighteen years, be loosed from this bond on the Sabbath day?" And the enemies of our Lord were ashamed when they heard his wise answer, and the people around wondered at his wisdom.

CHAPTER LX.

CHRIST WEEPS OVER JERUSALEM.

Grandma: One day, as Christ neared Jerusalem, looking down on the city from one of the surrounding hills he wept, saying: "Jerusalem, Jerusalem, thou that killest the prophets, and stonest them that are sent to thee, how often would I have gathered thy children, as the hen doth her brood under her wings, and thou wouldst not."

Paul: Grandma, what means to stone?

Grandma: To stone was to put to death; to kill by throwing stones at the victim. This was a means of torture among the Jews.

Jane: Why does our Lord say he would have gathered the children of Jerusalem under his wings?

Grandma: Our Lord sighed and wept over Jerusalem with these sad words, because Jerusalem being the capital of Judea, the place where the Jews gathered, our Lord had many times gone thither to instruct the Jewish people and to deliver them from the power of the evil one; to bring them salvation; to teach them the truth; and they would not listen to him. Then he added these words, predicting the downfall of Jerusalem: "Your houses shall be deserted; you shall not see me till you shall say: Blessed be he that cometh in the name of the Lord."

CHAPTER LXI.

A PARABLE ON HUMILITY.

Grandma: One day Jesus was invited to the house of a Pharisee to take dinner; and seeing that the guests who were invited were disputing among themselves as to who should have the first seat, he gave them a lesson in humility, saying:

"When thou art invited to a wedding, sit not down in the first place, lest perhaps one more honorable than thou be invited by him; and he that invited thee and him, come and say to thee: Give this man place; and then thou begin with shame to take the lowest place. But when thou art invited, go, sit down in the lowest place; that when he who invited thee cometh, he may say to thee: Friend, go up higher. Then shalt thou have glory before them that sit at table with thee. Because every one that exalteth himself, shall be humbled; and he that humbleth himself, shall be exalted."

Peter: Grandma, I don't see that this is a lesson in humility. It seems to me an example of pride.

Grandma: Where do you see pride, little one?

Peter: Our Lord tells them when they are invited they must not take the first place, but must take the last place.   He don't say to do this through humility, but that the master of the feast may give them a better place.

Grandma: This parable is a comparison, and comparisons are never perfect.   But if you listen carefully, and try to follow our Lord's thought, you will see that he wants to teach principally that they should not choose the first places.   He tells them that all men who strive to be exalted will be humbled before God, and often also before men.

Our Lord spoke also to his host, and said to him: "When thou maketh a dinner or a supper, call not thy friends, nor thy brethren, nor thy kinsmen, nor thy neighbors who are rich; lest perhaps they also invite thee again, and a recompense be made to thee. But when thou makest a feast, call the poor, the maimed, the lame, and the blind.   And thou shalt be blessed, because they have not wherewith to make thee recompense; for recompense shall be made thee at the resurrection of the just."

Henrietta: Then, Grandma, why do you invite us to dinner, and the ladies and gentlemen of the neighborhood who are rich and ask you to dine with them?   Why don't you invite the poor of the village?

Grandma: Our Lord does not forbid us to show hospitality to our kinsmen and to the rich.   He teaches us that we must never do good in order to receive a reward.   He uses dinners and feasts to represent all kinds of courtesies and kind services, which he wants us to give all men, not that they may return these kindnesses to us, but to obey the command of God. He also teaches us we must desire reward only from God and God alone.

CHAPTER XLII.

PARABLE OF THE FEAST.

Grandma: One of the guests seated at the table, whom the Gospel does not name, said to our Lord: "Blessed is he that shall eat bread in the kingdom of God."

To whom our Lord replied by another parable. "A certain man made a great supper, and invited many. And he sent his servant at the hour of supper to say to them that were invited, that they should come, for now all things are ready. And they began all at once to make excuse. The first said to him: I have bought a farm, and I must needs go out and see it; I pray thee, hold me excused. And another said: I have bought five yoke of oxen, and I go to try them; I pray thee, hold me excused. And another said: I have married a wife, and therefore I cannot come. And the servant returning told these things to his lord. Then the master of the house, being angry, said to his servant: Go out quickly into the streets and lanes of the city, and bring in hither the poor, and the feeble, and the blind, and the lame. And the servant said: Lord, it is done as thou hast com-

manded, and yet there is room. And the Lord said
to the servant: Go out into the highways and hed-
ges, and compel them to come in, that my house may
be filled. But I say unto you, that none of those
men that were invited shall taste of my supper."

Jack: What does our Lord mean by this parable?
Must we really compel people to come to our feasts,
when the invited ones don't come?

Grandma: No, dear child; this parable signifies
the feast to which we are one and all invited—to the
joys of paradise; to the kingdom of heaven. Our
Lord gives this parable in reply to the guest who
speaks of the feast in the kingdom of God, and of
the happiness of being gathered there.

The meaning is this: the Jews were the first
who had the happiness of being invited to this kingdom; the first bidden to sit at their Father's table.
However, instead of accepting with gladness, they
let themselves be led away by the pleasures of this
world, even as we do to-day. One has not the time
to serve God, he has too many things to see to;
another has pleasures, balls, parties, which fill every
hour of his day. Another has interesting books,
charming friends, worldly pursuits, which take up
his time so fully, he has not a moment free for God's
service. Another is delicate and has a large family,
and so on. The Master, who is God, sends his
servants, the priests, to warn them, to tell them that
the feast is spread, that they must hold themselves

in readiness to reply to our Lord's invitation. They do not harken to God's call, they refuse to hear the voice of the priests. Then God sends his ministers to foreign shores to convert the heathens and pagans. These heed the voice of God's messengers, and come in large numbers to the heavenly banquet. That is to say, these are converted and learn the truths of God's kingdom.

CHAPTER LXIII.

WE ARE TO LOVE GOD ABOVE ALL.

Grandma: One day as our Lord was walking, followed by a large crowd, he turned and said to them: "If any man come to me, and hate not his father, and mother, and wife, and children, and brethren, and sisters, yea, and his own life also, he cannot be my disciple."

Jane: Grandma, that would be wrong, it seems to me, to hate our relations.

Grandma: You forget that our Lord speaks figuratively, as when he speaks of cutting off our hands and our feet, if they are to us an occasion of sin. Our Lord here means that if we wish to be his friends and disciples, we must fear sin and avoid temptation with such care that if it came to us, even through our parents and those we love best, we must turn from them, in spite of the love we bear them and the respect we owe them.

Louis: Grandma, how could evil come to us from our parents and sisters and brothers?

Grandma: In the early centuries, after the coming of Christ—

Paul: What are centuries?

Grandma: A century is one hundred years.   In these first centuries the Roman emperors martyred the Christians.

Henry: What is martyred?

Grandma: Martyred means put to death for truth's sake.   The Roman emperors forbade the Christians to believe in Christ Jesus, and in order to force them to deny Christ and adore idols, they tortured them, martyred them most cruelly.   These noble Christians preferred to die in torments rather than to deny their faith in Christ.   They are, therefore, called martyrs.

To reply to Louis, I add that in these early days the first Christians had to obey our Lord's command of hating father and mother, in order to follow him. For their pagan parents and friends, not believing in Christ, tempted these martyrs to deny Christ, that their lives might be spared.

The martyrs turned away from the entreaties of those most dear to them, and for the love of Christ fled from the love of father, mother, sister, and brother, rather than deny Jesus.   Now and always we must obey Christ Jesus, even if we have to give up our most beloved friends, our most tender affections.   This is to love our Lord above all things.

Our Lord added: "And whosoever doth not carry his cross and come after me, is not worthy of me."

Jane: How can we carry a cross and follow Jesus?

Grandma: It is as if our Lord said to us: He who does not conquer his evil habits, he who does not bear with resignation the trials of this life, he who does not sacrifice pleasure to duty, and follow me, by imitating my charity, meekness, and patience, such a one cannot be my disciple, such a one cannot enter the kingdom of heaven.

196 The Life of Christ for Children

CHAPTER LXIV.

PARABLE OF THE GOOD SHEPHERD AND OF THE LOST GROAT.

Grandma: The Publicans and sinners drew near to Jesus to hear his words. "And the Pharisees and scribes murmured, saying: This man receiveth sinners, and eateth with them."

And turning to these men Christ spoke to them this parable: "What man of you that hath an hundred sheep: and if he shall lose one of them, doth he not leave the ninety-nine in the desert, and go after that which was lost, until he find it? And when he hath found it, lay it upon his shoulders, rejoicing; and coming home, call together his friends and neighbors, saying to them: Rejoice with me, because I have found my sheep that was lost? I say to you, that even so there shall be joy in heaven upon one sinner that doth penance, more than upon ninety-nine just who need not penance. Or what woman having ten groats—"

Paul: What is a groat?

Grandma: A groat is a silver piece worth about ten cents of our money. Our Lord said: "What woman having ten groats, if she lose one groat doth not light a candle, and sweep the house, and seek diligently until she find it? And when she hath found it, call together her friends and neighbors, saying to them: Rejoice with me, because I have found the groat which I had lost?"

And looking tenderly on the sinners, who were listening eagerly, our Lord added: "So I say to you, there shall be joy before the angels of God upon one sinner doing penance."

CHAPTER LXV.

THE PRODIGAL SON.

Grandma: Christ gave still another parable to show the mercy of God for repentant sinners. Still addressing the multitude, among whom were doubtless many sinners, our Lord said: "A certain man had two sons; and the younger of them said to his father: Father, give me the portion of substance that falleth to me. And he devided unto them his substance. And not many days after, the younger son went abroad into a far country, and there wasted his substance, living riotously. And after he has spent all, there came a mighty famine in that country."

Paul: What is a famine?

Grandma: A famine is a time of such scarcity of food that every one is hungry. The corn and the wheat have failed and there is little or no food for any one. Well, in that country there was a famine and he began to suffer with hunger; and he hired himself out on a farm to feed the swine. Willingly he would have eaten the food given to the hogs, for no one gave him anything to eat. And he thought to himself: "How many hired servants in my father's house abound with bread, and I here perish with hunger? I will arise, and will go to my father, and say to him: Father, I have sinned against heaven, and before thee. I am not now worthy to be called thy son; make me as one of thy hired servants."

"And rising up he came to his father. And when he was yet a great way off, his father saw him, and was moved with compassion, and running to him fell upon his neck and kissed him. And the son said to him: Father, I have sinned against heaven, and before thee. I am not now worthy to be called thy son."

But the father only answered by embracing him, and said to the servants: "Bring forth quickly the first robe and put it on him, and put a ring on his hand and shoes on his feet; and bring hither the fatted calf and kill it, and let us eat and make merry, because this my son was dead, and is come to life again; was lost, and is found. And they began to be merry."

Jack: How happy that son must have been! I wonder if I ran away and spent all my money, if my father would treat me that way if I came back?

Grandma: Perhaps he would, because he is a very good father; but perhaps he would not be so forgiving, for though a very good father, he is not as good as the Good God. This parable speaks of God, our heavenly Father, of his goodness to us.

sinful men. First our Lord tells us of the son, happy in his father's house, but who believes he would be happier far from home.

This may be a description of any one of us. We live happily under the law of God. Some day we are tempted to believe that far from God and the restraint of his law we may be happier. We give up our prayers, our good habits, the practice of virtue; we are led away by the pleasures of this world and we withdraw from God. We waste our health, our fortune, and our happiness in all kinds of worldly follies. When we are unhappy and the world thrusts us aside, when we suffer from want of love and of sympathy, then we recall our former happiness, and the peace of conscience we enjoyed when we were innocent. And if we have the courage, we make a brave resolve to leave this strange land, which is indeed a strange land to all good Christians, and to return to God, our Father.

We leave, therefore, this country with its people, which are our sins and vices; we go to our Father; we humble ourselves, we confess our sins, we acknowledge we are unworthy of his forgiveness. Our heavenly Father, instead of driving us from him, runs to meet us, that is to say, helps our repentance, gives us the grace to be humble. He gives us back our place among his servants and faithful friends. among good Christians. He invites us to his table of Holy Communion, and feeds us with his own body and blood. All the past is forgiven and forgotten.

This parable is called: "The Prodigal Son," and perhaps more than any other parable expresses the great goodness and great mercy of God. If any one of you, but I hope, indeed, you never will, offend God, our Father, like this prodigal son, do not lose courage. Remember that God is infinitely good, recognize your faults, pray God's pardon and confess them humbly and sincerely. The good God will open wide his arms and heart to you and will give you back your lost peace and joy.

When the prodigal son came home, his elder brother was in the field, "and when he drew nigh to the house, he heard music and dancing. And he called one of the servants, and asked what these things meant. And he said to him Thy brother is come, and thy father hath killed the fatted calf, because he hath received him safe. And he was angry and would not go in. His father, therefore, coming out began to entreat him. And he answering, said to his father: Behold, for so many years do I serve thee, and I have never transgressed thy commandment, and yet thou hast never given me a kid to make merry with my friends. But as soon as this thy son is come, who hath devoured his substance, thou hast killed for him the fatted calf. But he said to him: Son, thou art always with me, and all I have is thine. But it was fit we should make merry and be glad, for this thy brother was dead, and is come to life again; he was lost, and is found."

Jack: If I had been in that father's place I would have been very angry with that son who is jealous because his brother, who comes back repentant and unhappy, is so well received.

Grandma: The good father in the parable represents God our Father, who is more forgiving, more tender than you would ever be, my little Jack. He reproves the son with kindness. In the parable you see he leaves the hall of feasting to ask his son to come in; he listens to him with patience; he explains to him why he receives the brother with so much joy. Here also, in the dealings of the father with his eldest son, our Lord shows us the patience and goodness of our heavenly Father in dealing with us.

See how patiently he bears with us, how lovingly he treats us. He waits for us, and when we come back to him, he rewards us, as if we had never offended him.

CHAPTER LXVI.

PARABLE OF THE RICH MAN AND LAZARUS.

Grandma: One day, addressing the Pharisees, Jesus spoke to them this parable: "There was a certain rich man, who was clothed in purple and fine linen—"

Paul: What is purple?

Grandma: It was a very rare and very beautiful material, which was woven of threads dyed with that precious color. Our Lord by this discription indicates the man was rich and wore costly garments.

And our Lord added how "each day he fared sumptuously. And there was a certain beggar, named Lazarus, who lay at his gate, full of sores, and desiring to be fed with the crumbs that fell from the rich man's table, and no one did give him any. Moreover, the dogs came and licked his sores. And it came to pass, that the beggar died and was carried by the angels into Abraham's bosom."

Elizabeth: What does that mean, Grandma?

Grandma: It is an expression which means the kingdom of heaven, where the beggar was carried. to be happy eternally.

"And the rich man also died; and he was buried in hell. And lifting up his eyes when he was in torments, he saw Abraham afar off, and Lazarus in his bosom; and he cried, and said: Father Abraham, have mercy on me, and send me Lazarus, that he may dip the tip of his finger in water, to cool my tongue; for I am tormented in this flame. And Abraham said to him: Son, remember that thou didst receive good things in thy lifetime, and likewise Lazarus evil things, but now he is comforted, and thou art tormented.

"And besides all this, between us and you there is fixed a great chaos; so that they who would pass from hence to you, cannot, nor from thence come hither.

"And he said: Then, Father, I beseech thee, that thou wouldst send him to my father's house, for I have five brethren, that he may testify to them, lest they also come into this place of torments.

"And Abraham said to him: They have Moses and the prophets; let them hear them. But he answered: No, Father Abraham; but if one went to them from the dead, they will do penance. And he said to him: If they hear not Moses and the prophets, neither will they believe if one rise again from the dead."

Madeleine: This is a terrible parable.

Grandma: Yes; terrible for the rich who do not use their wealth well, as there are, unfortunately, many. You see, our Lord does not say that the rich man was wicked or unjust, but only that he dressed gorgeously and ate sumptuously; that he lived in the midst of pleasures and luxury. He did not drive Lazarus from his gate where he lay, but he did not think of him, he did not succor him, he did not feed him. It was for this life of indolence and uselessness, for his indifference to the sufferings of Lazarus, that the rich man was cast into hell. The rich who live in opulence and do not give to the poor, but spend their wealth seeking pleasures, are described by this rich man.

Such people prepare for themselves an eternity of unhappiness in exchange for a few years of enjoyment here below. The rich man asks for a drop of water to refresh his parched tongue. This is denied him. He asks that the dead be sent to warn his brethren, but this also is refused, for these brothers had the means of knowing their duty. They heard the truths of God's kingdom preached by the prophets; and if they refused to believe God's messengers, they would not even believe if one risen from the dead had come to them.

Christ continued speaking to the multitude, and he converted many.

The Pharisees heard how the multitude praised Jesus, they saw the miracles that he did and the admiration in which the people held him. They grew daily more jealous and angry. They had decided among themselves to put Jesus to death, and they were seeking an occasion to condemn him.

CHAPTER LXVII.

THE PHARISEES SEEK TO LAY HOLD OF JESUS.

Grandma: On the last day of the Feast of the Tabernacles—

Louis: What was that feast?

Grandma: The Feast of the Tabernacles was instituted by the Jewish people, in remembrance of their journey in the desert, when they had fled from Egypt. It lasted eight days, and to recall to mind those days when they had dwelt in tents, the people of Jerusalem spent these days in tents made of the boughs of trees.

On the last day of this festival the Pharisees sent men to lay hold of our Lord and seize him while he spoke to the people. But Christ Jesus spoke so well, he inspired such love and confidence, that these men dared not apprehend him, and they returned to the head priest, saying. "Never did man speak like this man."

The Pharisees answered angrily: "Are you also seduced? Hath any one of the rulers believed in him, or of the Pharisees? But this multitude, that knoweth not the law, are accursed."

Jack: Were they accursed?

Grandma: No; but the Pharisees in their arrogant pride said this, for they considered that they alone had the right to teach.   Yet these simple people were nearer the truth than they.

This happens even in our day and everywhere. Men of science think themselves more learned and wise than the simple souls who are humbly studying the lives of the saints, and who, enlightened by God's spirit, have often a deeper knowledge than the wise of this world.

CHAPTER LXVIII.

THE SINFUL WOMAN.

Grandma: I shall now relate to you another instance of our Lord's great goodness and mercy. One day after having prayed on Mount Olivet, our Lord went to the temple to teach the people. The Scribes and Pharisees brought him a wicked woman who had deceived her husband. And they told our Lord how her evil ways had been found out, and said they: "Moses in the law commanded us to stone such a one; but what sayest Thou?"

Our Lord read their thoughts, and knew they had brought this woman to him not to consult him, but in an evil spirit, hoping to find cause of complaint against him. If he had ordered her to be stoned they would have accused him of cruelty; or of disobeying the law of Moses, if he had forgiven her.

"But Jesus, bowing himself down, wrote with his finger on the ground—"

Louis: What did our Lord write?

Grandma: The Gospel does not tell us, but as he read their evil hearts, it is supposed that Christ wrote, either sentences from the Scriptures condemning the hypocrisy of the Pharisees, or that he wrote in the sand the secret sins of these men.

As the Pharisees continued to question our Lord. "he lifted himself up and said to them: He that is without sin among you, let him first cast a stone at her. And again stooping down, he wrote on the ground. But they hearing this, went out one by one, beginning at the eldest."

Little Louis: Why was that? Why did the eldest go out first?

Grandma: Because the eldest were probably the most sinful.

And Jesus remained alone with this woman, who stood before him trembling. "Then Jesus, lifting himself, said to her: Woman, where are they that accused thee? Hath no man condemned thee?"

The woman replied humbly: "No man, Lord. And Jesus said: Neither will I condemn thee. Go, and now sin no more."

And those who heard this judgment admired the charity and goodness of Jesus.

Then Christ spoke to the people assembled in the temple. He told them he was the Messias, the Son of God, sent by his Father to save the world from sin. He showed them how blind of heart they were, who did not believe in his words, and who would not recognize in him the Messias. He recalled to their minds the good counsels he had given them, and which had stirred their hearts. He reminded them of the many miracles he had performed in their favor.

Alas, many of these Jews were so hard-hearted that, instead of being moved and touched by the words of Christ, they took up stones to stone him. "But Jesus hid himself and went out of the temple," unharmed, for the time had not yet come when he would lay down his life for all men.

CHAPTER LXIX.

CURE OF THE MAN BORN BLIND.

Grandma: "And passing by, Jesus saw a man, who was blind from his birth; and his disciples asked him: Master, who hath sinned, this man or his parents, that he should be born blind? Jesus answered: Neither hath this man sinned, nor his parents; but that the works of God should be made manifest in him. I must work the works of him that sent me, whilst it is day; the night cometh, when no man can work. As long as I am in the world, I am the light of the world.

"When he had said these things, he spat on the ground, and made clay of the spittle, and spread the clay upon the blind man's eyes, and said to to him: Go, wash in the pool of Siloe. . . He went and washed, and he came seeing."

Then all the people of the neighborhood and all those who had seen him, formerly blind and asking alms said: "Is not this he that sat and begged? Some said: This is he. But others said: No, but he is like him. But he said: I am he. They said therefore to him: How were thy eyes opened? He answered: That man that is called Jesus made clay, and anointed my eyes, and said to me: Go to the pool of Siloe and wash. And I went, and I washed, and I see. And they said to him: Where is he? He saith: I know not."

Hearing this miracle from the blind man they took him to the Pharisees that he himself might tell them of his cure. For it was on the Sabbath Day that Jesus had performed this miracle.

The Pharisees questioned the man as to his cure and he said: "He put clay upon my eyes, and I washed, and I see.

"Some therefore of the Pharisees said: This man is not of God, who keepeth not the Sabbath. But others said: How can a man that is a sinner do such miracles?"

And they disputed among themselves, and turning to the blind man asked him: "What sayest thou of him that hath opened thy eyes? And he said: He is a prophet."

The Jews would not believe that this man had been born blind until they called his parents and questioned them. They asked the parents: "Is this your son who you say was born blind? How then doth he now see? His parents answered them and said: We know that this is our son, and that he was born blind; but how he now seeth, we know not; or who hath opened his eyes, we know not; ask him, he is of age let him speak for himself."

This his parents said because they feared the Jews,

for the Pharisees had agreed among themselves that
any one who would acknowledge Jesus to be Christ,
the Messias, would be driven out of the synagogue.

Henry: What did it matter to be driven out of
the synagogue?

Grandma: It was a shame, a disgrace, a malediction. The same as an excommunication would
be to-day; a decision which would drive us out of
the Church and would be a great disgrace to us.

The Pharisees therefore called again this man born
blind and said to him: "Give glory to God. We
know that this man is a sinner."

The blind man replied: "If he be a sinner, I
know not; one thing I know, that whereas I was blind
now I see. They said then to him: What did he to
thee? How did he open thy eyes? He answered
them: I have told you already, and you have
heard; why would you hear it again? Will you also
become his disciples?"

At this question they mocked him saying: "Be
thou his disciple, but we are the disciples of Moses.
We know that God spoke to Moses; but as to this
man, we know not from whence he is."

The blind man answered: "Why, herein is a
wonderful thing, that you know not from whence he
is, and he hath opened my eyes. Now we know
that God doth not hear sinners; but if a man be a
server of God, and doth his will, him he heareth.
From the beginning of the world it hath not been

heard that any man hath opened the eyes of one born blind. Unless this man were of God, he could not do anything. They answered, and said to him: Thou wast wholly born in sins, and dost thou teach us?" And they drove him out of the synagogue.

"Jesus heard that they had cast him out," and he went to seek him. "When he had found him he said to him: Dost thou believe in the Son of God? He answered, and said: Who is he, Lord, that I may believe in him? And Jesus said to him: Thou hast seen him, and it is he that talketh with thee. And he said: I believe, Lord. And falling down, he adored him."

Jack: That's good, I like that blind man. He is grateful and brave.

Henry: And how bad and untruthful those Pharisees are. They pretend not to believe in the power of our Lord.

Elizabeth: And this poor blind man, ignorant as he was, reasoned better than the wise Doctors of the Law. He hastened to recognize and adore our Lord.

Grandma: And therefore Jesus said, addressing him especially: "For judgment I am come into this world; that they who see not, may see; and they who see, may become blind."

Louis: What does that mean?

Grandma: It means our Lord came to enlighten those who, from ignorance, did not see the truth.

And they who, through pride, thought themselves capable of seeing the truth, without God's help, would remain blind of heart.

The Pharisees who were there and who heard these words, said mockingly: "Are we also blind? Jesus said to them: If you were blind, you should not have sin; but now you say: We see. Your sin remaineth."

Louis: What did our Lord mean?

Grandma: Our Lord meant that if the Pharisees had had more humility, they would have seen that they were blind and ignorant, and would, therefore, have asked for sight. But their pride prevented them from acknowledging their ignorance and asking for faith. For this reason Jesus Christ did not grant them sight, and they remained in sin, blind to the truth.

CHAPTER LXX.

THE GOOD SHEPHERD.

Grandma: And our Lord, still teaching the Pharisees and the multitude, said: "I am the good shepherd. The good shepherd giveth his life for his sheep. But the hireling—"

Paul: What is a hireling?

Grandma: A hireling is one who is paid for his services. The shepherd boy is hired and paid to care for the sheep.

Our Lord compared the shepherd, the owner and master of the flock, to the shepherd whom the master hired, and he said: "But the hireling, and he who is not the shepherd, whose own the sheep are not, seeth the wolf coming, and leaveth the sheep and flieth; and the wolf catcheth and scattereth the sheep. And the hireling flieth, because he is a hireling, and he hath no care for the sheep. I am the good shepherd, and I know mine, and mine know me. As the Father knoweth me, and I know the Father; and I lay down my life for my sheep.

"And other sheep I have, that are not of this fold; them also I must bring, and they shall hear my voice, and there shall be one Fold and one Shepherd.

Therefore doth my Father love me, because I lay
down my life, that I may take it again.   No man
taketh it from me; but I lay it down of myself, and
I have power to lay it down; and I have power to
take it up again."

Henrietta: Why does our Lord say he has other
sheep.   Where are they?

Grandma: The sheep to whom our Lord refers
are the pagans.   To these sheep Christ sent his
Apostles and their successors, the bishops and priests
of the Church, to convert them to the true Faith.
These then became Christians, and are therefore of
the same fold as the people of Israel, who believe in
Christ, and to whom our Lord was then speaking.

CHAPTER LXXI.

THE TEN LEPERS.

Grandma: Jesus on his way to Jerusalem passed through Samaria and Galilee. As he neared a small village, he was met by ten lepers. "They stood afar off and—"

Jane: Why did they stand far from our Lord?

Grandma: Because the lepers were forbidden to come into the villages and towns, or even draw near to those who passed by, for fear of giving them the leprosy, which is a very contagious malady, as I believe I have already told you.

These lepers, having stopped at a distance from Christ, lifted up their voice, saying: "Jesus, master, have mercy on us."

When Jesus saw them, he said to them: "Go, show yourselves to the priests."

And as they went on the way they were cured. One of them, when he saw he was made clean, went back, with a loud voice glorifying God.

And he fell on his face at the feet of Jesus, giving him thanks. And this leper was a Samaritan.

Then Jesus said: "Were not ten made clean? and where are the nine? There is no one found to return and give glory to God, but this stranger."

And Christ said to the grateful leper: "Arise, go thy way; for thy faith hath made thee whole."

CHAPTER LXXII.

THE PHARISEE AND THE PUBLICAN.
CHRIST BLESSES LITTLE CHILDREN.

Grandma: Our Lord gave the following parable to show that we must not have a good opinion of ourselves and despise others: "Two men went up into the temple to pray: the one a Pharisee, the other a publican. The Pharisee, standing, prayed thus with himself: O God, I gave thee thanks that I am not as the rest of men, extortioners, unjust, adulterers, as also is this publican. I fast twice in a week; I give a tenth of all that I possess. And the publican, standing afar off, would not so much as lift up his eyes towards heaven; but struck his breast, saying: O God, be merciful to me a sinner."

And Christ added that the humble publican had returned to his house forgiven; but not so the Pharisee, who had made his prayer in such a proud spirit; for, said Christ: "Every one that exalteth himself, shall be humbled; and he that humbleth himself, shall be exalted."

When he had finished speaking, they brought to him the little children, that he might bless them.

His disciples rebuked those who brought these little ones to Jesus, and would have driven them away from our Lord.

When Jesus saw this, he was much displeased; and he called the children to him and said: "Suffer the little children to come to me, and forbid them not; for of such is the kingdom of heaven. Amen, I say to you: whosoever shall not receive the kingdom of God as a little child, shall not enter into it."

Jack: But, Grandma, *you* can't become a little child again; and so you will not be able to go to heaven, nor any grown person!

Grandma: (laughing): Indeed, I hope to enter heaven some day, little one. Our Lord speaks of the innocence of children, not of their age. He wants us to be pure of all evil; innocent like little children, who never offend God. But when a child reaches the age of reason, which is supposed to be at seven years, he then knows right from wrong, and he may unfortunately offend God. However, if he confesses his sins, and is forgiven through the absolution he receives from the priest, he is once more innocent and pure.

When the children had been dismissed, the Jews questioned Christ, asking who he was. Christ answered clearly that he was the Son of God, sent by his father to save those who would believe in him and who would keep his commandments. He told them that he and his Father were One. But the

Jews, unwilling to believe that Jesus was Christ, the Son of God, at these words, took up stones to stone him, but he escaped from them unharmed.

CHAPTER LXXIII.

CHRIST AND THE RICH YOUNG MAN.

Grandma: One day, as our Lord set out on his daily journeying to preach God's kingdom, a rich young man ran up to him, "and kneeling before him, asked him: Good Master, what shall I do to possess everlasting life?"

Jesus answered him: "If thou wilt enter into life, keep the commandments."

And the young man asked which he should keep. And Jesus answered by enumerating the commandments:

"Thou shalt do no murder; thou shalt not commit adultery; thou shalt not steal, thou shalt not bear false witness; honor thy father and thy mother; and thou shalt love thy neighbor as thyself. The young man said to him· All these have I kept from my youth, what is yet wanting to me."

Jesus looked at this young man, so eager to do better, and he loved him; and Jesus said to him: "If thou wilt be perfect, go sell what thou hast, and give it to the poor, and thou shalt have treasure in heaven; and come follow me. And when the young man had heard this he went away sad, for he had great possessions."

Henrietta: Why does our Lord want this young man to sell all his possessions? It is not wrong to be rich.

Grandma: Our Lord does not, in this instance, command; he only counsels, advises. This young man desired to reach perfection. From his youth he had kept the commandments, and yet he goes to Christ with eagerness, asking what he shall do for eternal life. For this reason Christ loved him, for in him he saw the pure heart longing to do even more than the law commanded.

Therefore, our Lord counsels him to sacrifice the goods of this world and its pleasures, and to consecrate himself to God, as we see religious and priests doing every day. They give up all the riches of this world, all its comforts, in order to follow Christ more perfectly. And when our Lord saw that, in spite of his desires, the young man had not the courage to part with his wealth, he looked around and said: "How hardly shall they who have riches enter into the kingdom of God."

The disciples hearing this were greatly surprised. But Christ said a second time: "Children, how hard it is for them that trust in riches to enter into the kingdom of God. It is easier for a camel to pass through the eye of a needle than for a rich man to enter into the kingdom of God."

Henry: Why, Grandma, then the rich won't go to heaven?

Grandma: Our Lord only speaks of the rich who are selfish with their wealth, and who refuse to sacrifice their riches to God's will. For example, a good Christian would prefer to lose all his wealth, rather than keep it through some dishonest or unjust deed. On the other hand, the man who loves his riches more than the law of God, which leads to eternal life, would commit some selfish and unjust action to preserve his fortune.

The disciples were surprised, and asked a question very like Henry's: "Who, then, can be saved?" For they thought to themselves, no doubt, every one, unless he be a beggar, has some fortune. And Jesus, looking at them, said: "With men it is impossible; but not with God, for all things are possible with God. Then Peter said: Behold, we have left all things and have followed thee. What, therefore, shall we have? Jesus said to them: Amen, I say to you, that you, who have followed me, when the Son of man shall sit on the seat of his majesty, you also shall sit on twelve seats, judging the twelve tribes of Israel. And every one that hath left house, or brethren, or sisters, or father or mother, or wife, or children, or lands for my name's sake, shall receive an hundredfold, and shall possess life everlasting. And many that are first, shall be last and the last shall be first."

Louis: How is that, Grandma?

Grandma: That is to say that many who lead holy lives, and consequently seem destined to be first in the kingdom of heaven, if they do not persevere, may become wicked like Judas, who betrayed Christ.

And others who are wicked may be converted and become great saints, like St. Paul, who began by persecuting the Christians, and who became one of the greatest of the Apostles.

CHAPTER LXXIV.

PARABLE OF THE WORKMEN IN THE VINEYARD.

Grandma: To show the Jews how other nations of the earth, besides this chosen people, would receive the glad tidings of Christ's redemption, our Lord gave them the following parable:

"The kingdom of heaven is like to a householder, who went out early in the morning to hire laborers into his vineyard. And having agreed with the laborers for a penny a day, he sent them into his vineyard.

"And going out about the third hour, he saw others standing in the market place idle. And he said to them: Go you also into my vineyard, and I will give you what shall be just. And they went their way. And again he went out about the sixth and the ninth hour and did in like manner.

"But about the eleventh hour, he went out and found others standing, and he saith to them: Why stand you here all the day idle? They say to him: Because no man hath hired us. He saith to them: Go you also into my vineyard.

"And when evening was come, the lord of the vineyard saith to his steward: Call the laborers and pay them their hire, beginning from the last even to the first. When therefore they were come, that came about the eleventh hour, they received every man a penny. But when the first also came, they thought that they should receive more; and they also received every man a penny.

"And receiving it, they murmured against the master of the house, saying: These last have worked but one hour, and thou hast made them equal to us, that have borne the burden of the day and the heats. But he answering said to them: Friend, I do thee no wrong; didst thou not agree with me for a penny? Take what is thine and go thy way, I will also give to this last even as to thee. Or is it not lawful for me to do what I will? Is thy eye evil because I am good?

"So shall the last be first and the first last. For many are called, but few are chosen."

Elizabeth: Grandma, it seems to me that these laborers who had worked all day had a right to complain. They had worked twelve hours and the others one hour, and yet they did not receive any more than the last comers.

Grandma: Taken literally this parable seems strange at first sight; for those who had labored all day seem entitled to more pay than the last, who worked only a few hours. But it is not in this sense our Lord means this parable to be understood. He gives this parable to the Jews, to teach them that

God does them no injustice in giving to other
nations of the earth the happiness of knowing Jesus
Christ, the Savior of the world. The penny given
to all the laborers equally, to the last even as to the
first, represents Jesus Christ, who gives himself
with equal love to the Jews, to the pagans, and to all
men of good will. This penny promised as reward
by the Master, is our Lord promised to all men as
their Savior, from the beginning of the world.

Jack: And why don't the Master of the house
drive away those who murmur and complain?

Grandma: Because God is infinitely good, and
forgives their discontent, and even explains to them
the seeming injustice of which they complain; for he
says: "Is thy eye evil because I am good?"

Jane: What does that mean?

Grandma: Our Lord means that because I am
good to these men and reward their good will, you
must not be jealous and look upon this deed of mercy with an evil eye. After this parable Jesus predicted to his Apostles that he was going to Jerusalem,
where he would be delivered into the hands of the
high priest and the scribes; and that he would be
condemned to death, scourged, and crucified; but
that on the third day he would rise again from the
dead.

CHAPTER LXXV.

THE RAISING OF LAZARUS.

Grandma: There lived in the city of Bethany a good and wealthy man named Lazarus. He was the brother of Martha and of Mary. One day he fell ill. His sisters, who knew that Jesus loved him, sent messengers to say to our Lord: "He whom thou lovest is sick." Jesus said to those who brought the tidings of his friend's illness: "This sickness is not unto death, but for the glory of God; that the Son of God may be glorified by it."

Though Jesus loved Mary and Martha and Lazarus, having heard of their anxiety, he remained two days longer in the city where he was at that time. "Then, after that, he said to his disciples: Let us go into Judea again. The disciples say to him: Rabbi, the Jews but now sought to stone thee; and goest thou thither again?"

Then Jesus explained to them that the hour of his death, predicted by the prophets, had not yet come. He told them that nothing could prevent the approach of this hour; and nothing could hasten it; but he added: "Our friend Lazarus sleepeth; but I go that I may awake him out of sleep. His disciples, therefore, said   Lord, if he sleep, he shall do well.   But Jesus spoke of dis death; and they thought that he spoke of the repose of sleep.   Therefore Jesus said to them plainly: Lazarus is dead. And I am glad, for your sakes, that I was not there, that you may believe; but let us go to him."

Jack: Why was our Lord glad he was not there? He could have cured him and prevented his dying.

Grandma: Because our Lord knew he would raise him up from the dead; and he was glad that his disciples should witness such a miracle.

"Thomas, who is called Didymus, said to his fellow-disciples: Let us also go, that we may die with him."

You see, the disciples thought our Lord was in great danger in going to Jerusalem.

Jesus set out with his disciples; and soon reached Bethany, which is very near Jerusalem.   When they arrived, they found that Lazarus had died, and had been in the grave four days.

Many of the Jews had gathered round Martha and Mary, seeking to comfort these sisters in their great sorrow.

While Martha and Mary sat with their friends and relatives, grieving over their loss, word was brought to Martha that Jesus was approaching..

In all haste she went to meet him, and she said to him sadly: "Lord, if thou hadst been here, my brother had not died.   But now I know that whatsoever thou wilt ask of God, God will give it to thee. Jesus saith to her: Thy brother shall rise again. Martha saith to him: I know that he shall rise again, in the ressurection at the last day. Jesus said to her: I am the ressurection and the life; he that believeth in me, although he be dead, shall live; and every one that believeth in me shall not die forever. Believeth thou this? She saith to him: Yea, Lord, I have believed that thou art Christ the Son of the living God, who art come into this world.''

And when she had spoken thus with our Lord, she went and called her sister, whispering to her: ''The Master is come, and calleth for thee.''

Quickly Mary rose and hastened to Jesus, who had not yet entered the city, but was still on the outskirts of the town, where Martha had met him.

The Jews seeing Mary leave the house in great haste, thought she had gone to her brother's grave to weep, and they followed her.

When Mary met our Lord she fell at his feet; saying, as Martha had done: ''Lord, if thou hadst been here, my brother had not died.''

No doubt the two sisters had said this of our Lord to one another many times over in the past few days of sadness. When Jesus saw how Mary wept and also the friends and relatives who were with her, ''he groaned in spirit,'' and was deeply moved. And he asked: ''Where have you laid him?'' They replied: ''Come and see.'' ''And Jesus wept.''

Jack: Why did our Lord weep? If he loved Lazarus so much, why did he not save him? Then the poor sisters and their friends would not have been so sad and in so much trouble.

Grandma: Our Lord Jesus wept, for he was grieved at the grief of his friends. He shows us on this occasion that, far from blaming us, he sympathizes with the tears we shed at the loss of our parents and friends. Our Lord allowed Lazarus to die that he might perform the great miracle of raising him up from the dead, and thus prove his divine power to the Jews.

When the Jews saw Jesus weeping they said: "Behold how he loved him! But some of them said: Could not he that opened the eyes of the man born blind, have caused that this man should not die?"

Jesus reached the sepulchre where Lazarus was buried. It was a cave in front of which a large stone had been rolled. "Jesus saith: Take away the stone. Martha replied: Lord, by now he stinketh, for he is four days buried. Jesus saith to her: Did not I say to thee, that if thou believe, thou shalt see the glory of God? They took therefore the stone away. And Jesus, lifting up his eyes, said: Father, I give thee thanks that thou hast heard me. And I knew that thou hearest me always; but because of the people who stand about have I said it, that they may believe that thou hast sent me."

When he had thus prayed to his Father, "he cried out with a loud voice: Lazarus, come forth!" And immediately he that had been dead four days rose up alive out of the grave. His feet and hands and body were wrapped and bound in linen cloths, and his face was covered with a napkin. "Loose him," said our Lord, "and let him go."

Valentine: Grandma why was Lazarus wrapt and bound in cloths?

Grandma: It was the custom among the Jews to wrap the dead in linen bands and aromatic herbs. Over all these winding bands they folded a heavy winding sheet covering the dead from head to foot.

The Jews who witnessed this wonderful miracle, knew that no man could live four days in a tomb thus wrapped and swathed, and they knew they were looking on a man who had been dead, and who was now alive and well. Therefore, many of the Jews having seen what Jesus did, believed in him.

But several of these witnesses went to the Pharisees and told them what had happened. The Pharisees and High Priests assembled the Council to consult what they should do, saying: "What do we, for this man doth many miracles? If we let him alone all will believe in him; and the Romans will come, and take away our place and our nation."

One of them named Caiphas, who was High Priest that year, said to them: "You know nothing. Neither do you consider that it is better that one man should die for the people, so that the whole nation perish not."

Louis: He was a wicked man, for he knew that Jesus was good and innocent.

Grandma: This he knew very well, and so did they all; but they feared that the Romans, hearing of the power of Christ and of his influence over the people, would grow jealous. And that they would send their soldiers to drive out the priests and the Pharisees, and all those whom they had appointed rulers over the Jewish people.

From that day forth the Pharisees and Doctors of the Law sought to put Jesus to death.

Jesus, knowing their intention, appeared no more among the Jews publicly; but he withdrew to a small town near the desert, called Ephrem with his disciples.

Elizabeth: Grandma, as our Lord knew he was to die, why did he withdraw to Ephrem?

Grandma: Because the hour of his death, predicted by the Prophets, had not yet come. His work on this earth was not finished. In the retirement of Ephrem he taught his disciples many things concerning the redemption of the world.

CHAPTER LXXVI.

JESUS FORETELLS HIS DEATH AND RESURRECTION.

Grandma: As Jesus set out on the road leading to Jerusalem, his disciples, filled with dismay, followed him with great fear.

Jane: Why were they surprised and why were they afraid?

Grandma: They were amazed to see Jesus going so fearlessly to Jerusalem, where he had predicted that suffering and death awaited him.

And yet they followed him, because they loved him, and were unwilling to leave him, but full of fear lest they also should be ill-treated and suffer death with him.

But Jesus, reading their thoughts, took the twelve Apostles apart, and told them again that what the Prophets had foretold concerning him would be fulfilled in Jerusalem. That he would be delivered to the High Priest and to the Scribes, and that they would condemn him to death; that he would be mocked, spat upon, scourged, and finally put to death; but that on the third day he would rise again from the dead. The disciples did not understand all

that he told them, their minds were not yet open.
Yet of all the prophecies foretelling the sufferings
and death of Christ, this one is the clearest and the
most exact.

As they neared the city of Jericho, our Lord cured
a man born blind, who sat by the wayside and cried
out: "Jesus, Son of David, have mercy on me!"

Jesus restored his sight and the blind man, now
seeing clearly, followed the Savior, in a loud voice
giving glory and thanks to God.

CHAPTER LXXVII.

ZACHEUS RECEIVES JESUS IN HIS HOUSE.

Grandma: Jesus, entering Jericho, crossed the city. Here there dwelt a man named Zacheus, who earnestly desired to see and to know Jesus Christ. Zacheus was a rich man and head of the tax-collectors. Being very small and short, the crowd prevented him from seeing Jesus or drawing near to him. In his eagerness, running on ahead, he climbed into a sycamore tree, which grew on the roadside where Jesus was passing. As Christ reached the spot he raised his eyes and, calling Zacheus by name, he said: "Zacheus, make haste and come down; for to-day I must lodge in thy house."

Zacheus hastened to obey, and conducted our Lord to his home and received him with much joy.

The Jews seeing this, murmured among themselves, saying: "He is going to lodge in the house of a sinner."

But Zacheus, full of deep humility, standing respectfully before our Lord, said to him before all the people: "Lord, behold, now I give the half of my goods to the poor; and if I have wronged any man of anything, I restore it to him fourfold."

And Jesus answered; "This day is salvation come to this house, for the Son of Man is come to seek and to save that which was lost."

Jane: I don't understand, Grandma, why does our Lord say he came "to seek what was lost?" And why does Zacheus wish to give up all he has and return more than he has taken?

Grandma: Our Lord here speaks of the soul which can easily be lost through sin and love of riches; and these souls he came to save. Zacheus wished to give a portion of his wealth to make reparation for the deeds of injustice he had committed in compelling the payments of sums larger than were due. No doubt, you recall that the publicans collected the taxes due by the people to the State, and often they enforced payments that were unjust.

To atone, to do penance, for this injustice, Zacheus promises to return four times as much as he has unjustly received. This good resolution, which proved his sincere repentance, deserved for Zacheus our Lord's blessed assurance that his visit had brought to this house salvation and peace.

Jesus added the following parable before leaving the house of Zacheus.

CHAPTER LXXVIII.

PARABLE OF THE TEN TALENTS.

Grandma: "A certain nobleman went into a far country to receive for himself a kingdom, and to return. And calling his ten servants, he gave them ten pounds, and said to them: Trade till I come."

Paul: That does not seem much money for a king to give.

Grandma: In those days one pound, or talent, represented a large sum. Moreover, this king owed his servants nothing; he gave them this sum to test their faithfulness and ability to use it to the best advantage.

"But his citizens hated him; and they sent an embassy after him saying: We will not have this man to reign over us.

"And it came to pass that he returned, having received the kingdom; and he commanded his servants to be called, to whom he had given the money, that he might know how much every man had gained by trading.

"And the first came, saying: Lord, thy pound hath gained ten pounds.

"And he said to him: Well done, thou good and

faithful servant, because thou hast been faithful in a little, thou shalt have power over ten cities.

"And the second came, saying: Lord, thy pound gained five pounds.

"And he said to him: Be thou also over five cities.

"And another came, saying: Lord, behold here is thy pound, which I have kept laid up in a napkin; for I feared thee, because thou art an austere man; thou takest up what thou didst not lay down, and thou reapest that which thou didst not sow.

"He saith to him: Out of thy own mouth I judge thee, thou wicked servant. Thou knewest that I was an austere man, taking up what I laid not down, and reaping that which I did not sow; and why, then, didst thou not give my money into the bank, that at my coming I might have exacted it with interest? And he said to them that stood by: Take the pound away from him and give it to him that hath ten pounds. And they said to him: Lord, he hath ten pounds. But I say to you, that to every one that hath shall be given, and he shall abound; and from him that hath not, even that which he hath, shall be taken from him. But as for those my enemies, who would not have me reign over them, bring them hither and kill them before me."

Valentine: But what does this parable mean, Grandma? I can't imagine.

Grandma: The king here spoken of is the good God. The servants represent his creatures, mankind. The talents, or pounds, represent the various gifts which God distributed among men; such as, intelligence, cleverness, strength, courage, goodness, patience, kindliness, charity, and other qualities of mind and heart, of which there is an infinite variety.

The enemies of the king, who did not wish him to reign over them, are the Jews, who refused to recognize our Lord as their king.

The good servants, who turned to good account the money which their Master had confided to their care, are the wise and good, who earn for themselves great merit by the good use they make of the gifts of God.

The cities, which the king gives to his good servants represent the rewards that God will bestow upon us according to the work we have done for him, or the good we have accomplished, and the virtues we have acquired.

The wicked servant, who wraps his talent in a napkin, instead of striving to increase its value, represents those men who lose God's graces and his good gifts by allowing them to remain idle in their souls.

The bad citizens, in open revolt against the king whom they will not have to rule over them, are the Jews and all bad Christians who deny God and will

not repent and turn from evil to the good God.
The graces and gifts which they would not profit by
are given to the faithful and wise servants, who have
proved that they could appreciate and increase the
treasures confided to their care by their master,
the good Lord.

Our Lord, having finished this parable, continued
to journey towards Jerusalem and cured another
poor blind man who followed him on the way.

CHAPTER LXXIX.

MARY MAGDALENE ANOINTS THE FEET OF JESUS.

Grandma: Six days before the feast of the Passover Jesus stopped in Bethany where he had raised Lazarus from the dead and where dwelt the sisters of Lazarus, Martha and Mary. Martha served the evening meal and Lazarus sat at table with Christ, together with other invited guests.

Mary, full of reverence and love for the divine guest, took an alabaster vial of exquisite and precious perfume, and breaking the vase poured its contents over the feet of Christ. The house was filled with the fragrant odor of this ointment.

Then Judas Iscariot, one of the twelve Apostles, who sat at table, said: "Why was not this ointment sold for three hundred pence, and given to the poor?"

He said this, not because of charity for the poor, but because it was he who carried the purse, who had charge of the expenditures; and he used this money for his own purposes.

Jesus answered: "Let her alone, why do you molest her? She hath wrought a good work upon me. For the poor you have always with you; and whensoever you will, you may do them good; but me you have not always. She is come beforehand to anoint my body for the burial. Amen I say to you, wheresoever this gospel shall be preached in the whole world, that also which she hath done, shall be told for a memory of her."

The Jews having learnt of the presence of Jesus in Bethany, came in crowds to the house, not that they might see Jesus only, but Lazarus also, whom he had raised from the dead.

And because of this miracle many Jews believed in Christ. Therefore the chief priests sought means to put Lazarus to death, fearing his influence over the people.

BOOK FIFTH

Last Days in the Ministry of Jesus

CHAPTER LXXX.

THE TRIUMPHAL ENTRY OF JESUS INTO JERUSALEM.

Grandma: The next day our Lord continued his journey to Jerusalem. As he neared the village of Bethphage, he called to him two of his disciples and said to them: "Go into yonder village lying before us; upon your entrance you shall find an ass tied, and a colt with her, on which no man has ever yet mounted. Loose them and bring them to me. And if any one say to you: What are you doing? say: The Lord has need of them, and straightway he will let them go."

The disciples went before him to Bethphage and found the ass as Christ had told them, and when they untied her, those who stood by said: "What are you doing?"

They replied as Jesus had bidden them, and were allowed to take the ass and the young colt; and they led them to Jesus, who was waiting with the other disciples.

They spread their garments upon the back of the ass that Jesus might mount, and some of the people threw their mantles on the ground to make a path for the ass which carried the Savior; others, standing by, cut branches from the trees and strewed the ground with these green boughs.

And the disciples and the crowd who had gathered around shouted for joy, crying: "Hosanna, blessed is he that cometh in the name of the Lord. Hosanna to the Son of David. Hosanna in the highest." Then the Pharisees who stood by said to our Lord: "Silence thy disciples." But Jesus answered: "If these shall hold their peace, the stones shall cry out."

Little Louis: Grandma, how can stones cry out?

Grandma: Our Lord meant that the joy and enthusiasm of the people was so great that it would be impossible to silence them, and that nothing could prevent their joyful song of "Hosanna;" which means, "Glory to God," Whom they were praising because of the coming of Christ.

CHAPTER LXXXI.

JESUS WEEPS OVER JERUSALEM.

Grandma: As our Lord drew near to Jerusalem from the heights of Mount Olivet, He looked upon the city spread out before Him and He wept, saying: "If thou hadst known, in this thy day, the things that are to thy peace; but now they are hidden from thy eyes. For the days shall come upon thee; and thy enemies shall cast a trench about thee, and compass thee, and straiten thee on every side, and beat thee flat to the ground, and the children who are in thee; and they shall not leave in thee a stone upon a stone; because thou hast not known the time of thy visitation."

Elizabeth: Grandma, there are many things in these words of our Lord which I don't understand. Why does our Lord weep and grieve over the misfortunes of Jerusalem—when the Jews were so wicked towards Him? And who are these enemies of Jerusalem—and what means Jerusalem did not know "the time of her visitation?" Who visited her?

Grandma: Our Lord is grieved at the thought of the sorrows which he foresees will come upon

Jerusalem, because, in spite of the wickedness of the Jewish people, He loved them as he loves all men, and, moreover, they were His chosen people and he longed that they should know the truth and merit eternal life.   The enemies to which Christ refers are the Romans, a people who, forty years after the death of our Lord, overthrew Jerusalem, leaving not a stone upon a stone, as was predicted by our Lord.

This was the punishment of the Jewish people for their wilful blindness. They had witnessed the miracles of Christ, and they should have understood that these miracles proved Him to be the Messias long expected by their nation.   But the Jews feared that by the coming of Christ they might lose their power and might be compelled to obey instead of to command, that they would be condemned for their many faults; and, therefore, they made every effort to put to death the Messias, the Savior of the world.

In this effort they succeeded and then they sought to conceal His resurrection, as you will see later on. But, in spite of them, the glorious resurrection of Christ was made known and proved Christ Jesus to be the Son of God.

Therefore, does our Lord justly say that they refused to know the time of the visitation of their Redeemer, whose coming had long been looked for by the Jewish nation.

Our Lord spoke at length to the people.   He told them He would not ask His Father to deliver Him from the death which awaited Him, because for this purpose He had come into this world, and that by His death the devil would lose his power.

And Jesus added: "If I be lifted up from the earth, I will draw all things to Myself."

In these words He spoke of the cross to which He would be nailed, and which would be lifted up on Mount Calvary. He foretold that by His death many would be drawn to Him, and through Him they would be saved.

And some in the crowd listening to Him asked: "Who is this?"

And His friends answered with joy: "This is Jesus the prophet, from Nazareth of Galilee."

Little Louis: Was our Lord really a prophet?

Grandma: Our Lord was more than a prophet. He was the Lord and King of Prophets. Jesus entered the Temple and cured the lame and the blind, who came to Him that they might be healed. And the children cried out Hosanna to the Son of David."

Henrietta: What does Hosanna mean?

Grandma: Hosanna means glory—"Glory to the Son of David," sang the little children, praising God. The Pharisees, hearing them, were indignant and said: "Hearest Thou what these say?" Jesus answered: "Yea, have ye never read: Out of the mouths of infants thou hast perfected praise?"

And Jesus, leaving the people, went out of the city with His twelve disciples to Bethany where he was always welcome.

CHAPTER LXXXII.

JESUS CONDEMNS THE BARREN FIG TREE.—THE VENDERS DRIVEN FROM THE TEMPLE.

Grandma: After resting with His friends in Bethany, our Lord set out early the next day with His disciples for Jerusalem. As He journeyed on the road, He grew hungry, for you know our Lord, being man as well as God, was subject to all the needs of human nature.

It was not the season for figs, but seeing at a distance a fig tree in full leaf, He drew near and, pushing aside the leaves, He looked for the fruit, but in vain. He found only leaves; and addressing the fig tree He said: "May no fruit grow on thee any more forever."

Jack: But, Grandma, it doesn't seem to me it was the fault of the tree, as it was not the season for figs.

Grandma: The fig tree bears its leaves and its fruit at the same time. Therefore, as the tree was in full leaf, the passers by could expect to find fruit among the leaves. This tree presented, then, a false appearance and deceived the wayfarers. In condemning the fig tree, our Lord wished to give us, and those who heard Him, a lesson on the wickedness of hypocrisy, which leads men to *appear* better than they are; to appear to possess virtues which in reality they have not.

When He reached Jerusalem, our Lord entered the Temple. Here He found men selling sheep, lambs, and doves, and money changers changing silver and gold.

Full of holy indignation at this profanation of God's Temple, Christ drove out the buyers and sellers and overturned the tables of the money changers, saying: "My house shall be called the house of prayer; but you have made it a den of thieves." Thus He taught respect for His Father's house.

The sun having set, Jesus left the city.

CHAPTER LXXXIII.

CHRIST ANSWERS THE PHARISEES.

Grandma: The next day our Lord returned to Jerusalem. When again passing the fig tree, which He had condemned because it bore no fruit, the disciples saw that it was withered and dead. Our Lord again entered the Temple. The priests and Doctors of the Law drew near and said to Him: "Tell us by what authority Thou dost these things? and who hath given Thee this authority?"

Jesus answering, said to them: "I also will ask you one word, which if you shall tell Me, I will also tell you by what authority I do these things. Was John the Baptist a prophet sent from God or not?"

And they consulted among themselves what they should answer, and they argued: "If we say he was from heaven, He will say: Why, then, did you not believe him? If we say from men, the whole people will stone us; for they are persuaded John was a prophet."

Therefore they answered Jesus: "We know not."

And Jesus said to them: "Neither do I tell you by what authority I do these things."

Louis: Why would not our Lord tell them? He had so well answered them before.

Grandma: Because our Lord knew that His reply would do no good. They did not question Him to know the truth, but in the hope that He would say something in which they could find some fault.

CHAPTER LXXXIV.

PARABLE OF THE VINEYARD AND THE HUSBANDMEN.

Grandma: Our Lord spoke this parable to the people: "But what think you? A certain man had two sons; and coming to the first, he said: Son, go work to-day in my vineyard. And he answering said: I will not. But afterwards, being moved with repentance, he went. And coming to the other, he said in like manner. And he answering said: I go, Sir; and he went not. Which of the two did the father's will? They say to Him: The first."

And our Lord added that the sinners and the publicans, whom the Jews despised, would go into the kingdom of God before them; for these had believed in John the Baptist and turned from sin, whereas the preaching of John had left the Jews unmoved.

Jesus continued teaching in parables. "A certain man planted a vineyard, and let it out to husbandmen; and he went abroad for a long time. And at the season, he sent a servant to the husbandmen that they should give him of the fruit of the vineyard. Who, beating him, sent him away empty. And again

he sent another servant.   But they beat him also
and treating him reproachfully, sent him away
empty.   And again he sent a third; and they wounded
him also, and cast him out.

"And the Lord of the vineyard said: What shall
I do?   I will send my beloved son; it may be, when
they see him, they will reverence him.   Whom
when the husbandmen saw, they thought within
themselves, saying: This is the heir, let us kill him,
that the inheritance may be ours.

"So casting him out of the vineyard, they killed
him.   What, therefore, will the lord of the vineyard do to them?

"He will come, and he will destroy those husbandmen and he will give the vineyard to others."

Which the Jews hearing they said to our Lord:
"God forbid!"

Henry: Who are these husbandmen, Grandma;
and why do the Jews say: "God forbid?"

Grandma: The Master of the Vineyard is the
Good God.   *The Vineyard* is the Church, which bears
the fruits of faith, hope, and charity.   *The Husbandmen* are the Jewish people, to whose care God
had confided the truths of faith which they were to
spread over the whole world.   *The Servants* sent
to the husbandmen are the prophets, whom the Jews
drove from their midst, persecuted, and finally
killed.   *The Son of the King is,* of course, our Lord
whom the Jews likewise cast out of their synagogues

and put to death.   *The husbandmen* who received the vineyard which had been confided to such unworthy laborers are the Gentiles.

Louis: Who are the Gentiles?

Grandma: The word Gentile means the people outside of the Jewish nation.   The gift of faith was given to them.   They know and love Christ our Lord, whom the Jews dispised.

When our Lord had concluded this parable, the Jews cried out: "God forbid!" because they fully understood its meaning, and they feared the punishment our Lord foretold would befall their nation, if they presisted in rejecting the Messias who stood in their midst.

The priests and princes understood that these words of our Lord were addressed to them as a warning, for they were the teachers of the people.

Therefore, they sought to lay hold of Jesus, but they dared not, for fear of the people who honored Him.

CHAPTER LXXXV.

PARABLE OF THE WEDDING FEAST.

Grandma: Our Lord spoke to them the following parable: "The Kingdom of Heaven is likened to a king, who made a marriage for his son. And he sent his servants, to call them that were invited to the marriage; and they would not come. Again he sent other servants, saying: Tell them that were invited, Behold, I have prepared my dinner; my beeves and fatlings are killed, and all things are ready; come ye to the marriage.

"But they neglected, and went their ways, one to his farm, and another to his merchandise. And the rest laid hands on his servants and, having treated them contumeliously, put them to death.

"But when the king had heard of it, he was angry, and, sending his armies, he destroyed those murderers, and burnt their city. Then saith he to his servants. The marriage indeed is ready; but they that were invited were not worthy. Go ye therefore into the highways; and as many as you shall find, call to the marriage.

"And his servants, going forth into the ways, gathered together all that they found, both bad and good; and the marriage was filled with guests. And the king went in to see the guests; and he saw there a man who had not on a wedding garment. And he saith to him: Friend, how camest thou in hither not having on a wedding garment? But he was silent. Then the king said to the waiters. Bind his hands and his feet, and cast him into the exterior darkness; there shall be weeping and gnashing of teeth. For many are called, but few are chosen."

Louis: I don't understand this parable. What does this marriage feast mean? What king is it?

Grandma: In the parables of our Lord, the *king* always represents *God*. The *wedding* of the king's son represents the union of the Son of God, Christ Jesus, with our human nature, which He *wedded* in becoming man.

The *first guests* invited are the Jews, who were the *first* invited to the Feast of the Holy Eucharist. This great Feast of the Eucharist, in which our Lord Himself is our food, was instituted by Jesus at the last supper. The last supper of our Lord with His disciples was to take place in a few days, and I shall tell you shortly how, on this occasion, He showed His love for man.

The *servants* sent by the king are the *Apostles*, the *Disciples*, the *Priests*, the *Missionaries*, whom the world ill-treated and finally put to death.

The *armies* represent *wars*, *famines*, *plagues*, which are sent by God to chastise those who repulse

His servants and will not hear them.   The *man* who is found at table without a wedding garment is the picture of *those who* dare to approach the table of Eucharist and receive Holy Communion without having purified their soul by true contrition and sin-cere confession.

The *command* of the king, that the man without the wedding garment be bound hands and feet and cast into exterior darkness, is a sad but true representation of the *judgement* of God towards rebellious sinners who die with the stain of grievous sin upon their souls, and are therefore condemned to the pains of hell.

CHAPTER LXXXVI.

THE TRIBUTE TO CAESAR.

Grandma: The Pharisees withdrew to consult among themselves how they could best find some cause for taking our Lord prisoner.

They planned to put to our Lord some question concerning the Roman laws, and they hoped that in His reply He would speak against their Emperor, Caesar; and they would thus find a cause against Him. Therefore, they sent to Christ two spies to question Him concerning the tribute money which they paid to the Romans.

As if they were earnestly seeking to know the truth, these men came to Jesus, saying: "Master, we know that Thou speakest and teachest rightly; and Thou dost not respect any person, but teachest the way of God in truth. Is it lawful for us to give tribute to Caesar or not?"

But Jesus, knowing their wicked cunning, answered: "Why do you tempt Me, ye hypocrites? Bring me a penny that I may see it. And they brought it to Him and Jesus saith to them: Whose image and inscription is this? They say to him,

Caesar's. And Jesus answering, said to them Render, therefore, to Caesar the things that are Caesar's, and to God the things that are God's."

Elizabeth: How beautifully our Lord replies to these Jews who try to harm Him!

Henry: They could not answer anything to that. They must have been angry at being caught themselves.

Grandma: The Gospel tells us that, having heard this reply of our Lord, they were amazed, and went away wondering at His wisdom.

Henry: Were they converted?

Grandma: The Gospel does not say so. It is more probable that these men remained full of pride and envy, for it is impossible for men to repent when their hearts are full of hatred of their neighbor.

CHAPTER LXXXVII.

THE LOVE OF GOD AND OF OUR NEIGHBOR.

Grandma: The Pharisees were very angry when they learnt that Christ had silenced their messengers by His reply full of divine wisdom.

And one of the Doctors of the Law, hoping to succeed in confusing our Lord, drew near and asked Him which was the greatest of all the commandments. And Jesus answered: "Thou shalt love the Lord thy God with thy whole heart, and with thy whole soul, and with thy whole mind. This is the greatest and the first commandment. And the second is like to this: Thou shalt love thy neighbor as thyself. There is no other commandment greater than these."

Henry: But Grandma, there are *ten* commandments, and our Lord says there are two!

Grandma: Yes, God gave to Moses ten Commandments, which you have studied in your catechism. These two which Christ gives contain *all* the others: for He added: "On these two commandments dependeth the whole law."

If you keep this first commandment, of loving God, you honor Him, you adore Him, you obey Him. And if you love your neighbor as yourself, as this second commandment teaches, you are naturally kind, patient, charitable, and generous towards others. This love of God and of our neighbor for His sake, will make us as perfect as we can be in this world.

Camille: Grandma, how can we love everybody? How can I love those who hurt me as I love you? How can we love people who are cross and ill-tempered as we love those who are aimable and loving?

Grandma: Dear child, the good God does not compel us to love every one with the same affection. To love all men means to feel kindly towards everybody, to bear ill-will to no one, to be kind and charitable to all, to make allowances for the faults of others, to bear with them and pray for them. This is the love we must bear towards all—this is the law of love which Christ taught us.

Elizabeth: But, Grandma, if some one is unkind to me, and does me harm, I can't feel as kindly towards that person as if she were my friend.

Grandma: This is precisely where our *merit* lies. Our Lord demands of us this effort, not always easy, I admit, but which will win for us a great reward.

It is a pleasure to be kind to those we love and to those who love us; but to be kind towards our enemies, and to those who are cold and distant towards us, requires a great and generous effort. Our Lord asks this of all His followers, and He Himself gave us the example during all His life and especially in His sufferings and death, of which I shall presently tell you.

The Scribe who had questioned Christ saw the truth and beauty of this reply, and he exclaimed: "Master, you have well said;" and he repeated thoughtfully the words of Jesus, and spoke so earnestly that our Lord said to him: "Thou art not far from the Kingdom of God."

And no one dared question Christ further. As the Pharisees had gathered around our Lord, He turned and questioned them: "What think ye of Christ? Whose Son is He?"

"David's," they replied.

And our Lord asked: "How then doth David call Him Lord? If David called Him Lord, how is He his son?"

None could reply to this, and from that day they dared not question Him.

Louis: And we don't understand either, Grandma.

Grandma: However, it is very simple for all of you who know your catechism. Jesus Christ is the Lord of David, because He is true God, the Lord of all men. He is the son of David, because He is true man, and descended from David through His mother, the Blessed Virgin Mary. It is the mystery of the Incarnation, *God made man*, in which the Jews would not believe.

CHAPTER LXXXVIII.

THE WIDOW'S MITE.

Grandma: One day our Lord was sitting on the porch of the Temple, near the money box, placed there to receive the offerings of the people as they came in and out of the Temple.

As He watched the people giving their alms, a poor widow drew near and dropped in the box two small pieces of money worth less than one cent. Turning to His disciples our Lord said: "In truth, this poor widow has given more than all the others. For all they did cast in of their abundance; but she of her want cast in all she had, even her whole living."

Elizabeth: It certainly must be comforting to the poor to know that they too can give alms, and that if they can give only a little, it will deserve our Lord's praise.

CHAPTER LXXXIX.

JESUS PREDICTS THE RUIN OF JERUSALEM AND THE LAST DAY.

Grandma: Our Lord predicted the ruin of Jerusalem and that there would not be a stone left upon a stone of this city which the Jews loved. He foretold the end of the world, and predicted that before the last day Christians would be persecuted, and war, famine, floods, and plagues would devastate the earth, and that all these would be signs of the coming of Christ to judge the world. He told them that on the last day the Son of God would appear in His majesty, and that the dead should rise again and stand before Him to be judged. The good would be separated from the wicked; the wicked to be eternally punished and the good eternally rewarded according to their deeds.

Elizabeth: When will this be, Grandma?

Grandma: Our Lord did not reveal when the end of the world would come. This, He told them, was God's secret, which even the angels in Heaven did not know, but He warns us, as He warned His disciples, "to watch and pray," that we may be ready at any time to appear before God, "for no one knoweth the day and the hour" that he will be called to appear before his Judge.

CHAPTER XC.

PARABLE OF THE TEN VIRGINS.

Grandma: "The Kingdom of Heaven," said Jesus, "shall be like to ten virgins, who taking their lamps went out to meet the bridegroom and the bride. And five of them were foolish, and five wise. But the five foolish, having taken their lamps, did not take oil with them; but the wise took oil in their vessels with the lamps. And the bridegroom tarrying, they all slumbered and slept.

"And at midnight there was a cry made: Behold the bridegroom cometh, go ye forth to meet him. Then all those virgins arose and trimmed their lamps. And the foolish said to the wise: Give us of your oil, for our lamps are gone out. The wise answered, saying: Lest perhaps there be not enough for us and for you, go ye rather to them that sell, and buy for yourselves. Now, whilst they went to buy, the bridegroom came; and they that were ready went in with him to the marriage, and the door was shut.

"But at last come also the other virgins, saying: Lord, Lord, open to us. But He answering said: Amen I say to you, I know you not.

"Watch ye therefore, because you know not the day nor the hour."

Henry: Grandma, will you please explain this parable? I don't understand it.

Grandma: Most willingly. The *ten virgins* represent *Christians;* the *light* of their lamps is the *light* of faith; the *oil* is the *love* of God and *good deeds;* the *bridegroom* is *Christ Jesus.*

The virgins waited for the bridegroom, as all Christians await the last judgement; the sleep of the virgins represents death, and their awakening, the final resurrection, when each one of us will find in our lamps the oil poured in during our lives; that is, the good deeds done while on this earth.

The foolish virgins, who went to buy oil when they heard the bridegroom was approaching, represent those who wait until the last hour of their lives to do good and turn from sin. They have not the time to repent, and when these foolish Christians reach the door of the heavenly kingdom, they are too late, the door is shut. They had not purified their souls by sincere repentance and made friends with God during life, and death found them unprepared for His coming.

Therefore they are condemned and cannot enter the hall of feasting, which signifies Paradise.

"And," continued our Lord, "when the Son of Man shall come in His majesty, and all His angels with Him, then shall He sit upon the seat of His majesty. And all nations shall be gathered together before Him; and He shall separate them one from another, as the shepherd separateth the sheep from the goats. And He shall set the sheep on His right hand, but the goats on the left.

"Then shall the King say to them that shall be on His right hand: Come, ye blessed of My Father, possess you the kingdom prepared for you from the foundation of the world. For I was hungry, and you gave Me to eat; I was thirsty, and you gave Me to drink; I was a stranger, and you took me in; naked, and you covered me; sick, and you visited Me; I was in prison, and you came to Me.

"Then shall the just answer Him, saying: Lord, when did we see Thee hungry, and fed thee; thirsty, and gave Thee drink? And when did we see Thee a stranger, and took Thee in? or naked, and covered Thee? Or when did we see Thee sick or in prison, and came to Thee?

"And the King answering shall say to them: Amen, I say to you, as long as you did it to one of these My least brethren, you did it to Me.

"Then He shall say to them also that shall be on His left hand: Depart from Me, you cursed, into everlasting fire which was prepared for the devil and his angels. For I was hungry, and you gave Me not to eat; I was thirsty, and you gave Me not to drink; I was a stranger, and you took Me not in;

naked, and you covered Me not; sick and in prison, and you did not visit Me.

"Then they also shall answer Him, saying: Lord, when did we see Thee hungry, or thirsty, or a stranger, or naked, or sick, or in prison, and did not minister to Thee? Then He shall answer them, saying: Amen, I say to you, as long as you did it *not* to one of these least, neither did you it to Me. And these shall go into everlasting punishment; but the just into life everlasting."

Henry: But, Grandma, must we love the poor as we do God?

Grandma: Our Lord teaches us that all men, poor and rich, good and bad, are our brothers, and that for love of Him who became man we must treat all men as our brethren and His brethren; otherwise we cannot hope to be happy with Him in heaven.

When you read the lives of the saints you will see how they saw in the poor of this world our Lord Himself and how, for love of Him, they clothed them and fed them and ministered to their wants.

Jesus spent these last days of His life teaching the people, who assembled in large numbers to hear Him; and at night He would withdraw outside the city to the Mount of Olives to pray.

CHAPTER XCI.

JUDAS DETERMINES TO BETRAY CHRIST.

Grandma: Jesus being alone with His disciples said to them: "You know that after two days the Son of Man shall be delivered up to be crucified."

While our Lord was conversing thus with His disciples, the priests and scribes and ancients of the people had gathered together in the hall of Caiphas, the High Priest, and were consulting among themselves how they might lay hold of Jesus and put Him to death. They decided that this must not be on the festival day, lest there should be a tumult among the people, for they knew many loved the Christ, who had gone among them doing good.

While they were deliberating, "Satan entered into Judas," one of the twelve disciples.

Jack: How could Satan enter into Judas?

Grandma: Judas listened to the Evil One, who whispered that if he betrayed his Master he would be well paid by the enemies of Christ. This thought pleased Judas, who had grown to love riches, and he resolved to betray Jesus and sell Him to those who were seeking His death. From the moment Judas consented to this temptation he was in the power of the devil, who had entered into his heart. And he went immediately to the chief priests and princes and offered to deliver Jesus to them.

They accepted eagerly, for they did not know where Christ spent the night, and they bargained with Judas and agreed to pay him thirty pieces of silver when he would have betrayed Christ Jesus into their hands.

Jack: My, what a wicked man this Judas was! And he was one of the twelve Apostles; I wonder our Lord did not drive him away long ago!

Grandma: Our Lord came upon this earth to do the will of His Father and save men by his death. He left Judas free as to the use he would choose to make of the wonders of love and mercy which he witnessed in the Master's blessed company. Thus Christ obeyed the will of God Who leaves men their free will to turn from evil and do good in all the freedom of their own deliberate choice. Moreover, in all his dealings with Judas, His unworthy disciple, Christ gave us the most sublime example of perfect charity, patience, humility, and forgiveness of injuries, which virtues He had preached during His whole life.

Like Judas, unfaithful Christians leave our Lord and betray Him. Nevertheless, God is patient and grants them long years of life, that they may repent.

And like Judas they, too, are inexcusable if they are not moved to repentance and conversion from their sins.

CHAPTER XCII.

THE LAST SUPPER.

Grandma: The Feast of the Passover was drawing near, and on the day of the azymes.

Louis: What is the day of the azymes?

Grandma: During the Feast of the Passover the Jews ate only unleavened bread, bread without yeast called azymes. Therefore, the first day of the feast, which lasted seven days, was called the day of the azymes.

This day being at hand, Jesus said to Peter and to John: "Go, and prepare for us the pasch, that we may eat. But they said: Where wilt Thou that we go. But he said to them: Behold, as you go into the city, there shall meet you a man carrying a pitcher of water; follow him into the house where he entereth in. And you shall say to the good man of the house: The Master saith to thee, Where is the guest chamber, where I may eat the pasch with My disciples? And he will show you a large dining-room furnished; and there prepare ye for us."

The disciples did as our Lord commanded, and found everything precisely as He had told them; and they prepared the pasch.

Mary Theresa: What was there to prepare?

Grandma: Many things: First the lamb had to be killed and roasted. Then the unleavened bread and certain bitter herbs, which it was customary to eat with the lamb, had to be prepared. Then the table, spread with all that was needful for the paschal supper, as this repast was called. In the evening our Lord went up to Jerusalem.

Valentine: Why do you say, Grandma, that Jesus "went up" to Jerusalem?

Grandma: Because the city of Jerusalem was built on a height. After sunset our Lord sat down at table with His twelve disciples, and He said to them: "With desire I have desired to eat this pasch with you, before I suffer. For I say to you, from this time I will not eat it, till it be fulfilled in the Kingdom of God."

Then, taking the cup of wine, He gave thanks to His Father and said to His disciples: "Take, and divide it among you; for I say to you, I will not drink of the fruit of the vine, till the Kingdom of God come."

And while they were eating, our Lord spoke to them thus: "Amen I say to you, that one of you is about to betray Me."

At these words the disciples were much grieved and each one asked: "Lord, is it I?"

And our Lord answering said: "He that dippeth his hand with Me in the dish, he shall betray Me.

The Son of Man indeed goeth, as it is written of Him; but woe to that man by whom the Son of Man shall be betrayed; it were better for him, if that man had not been born."

And Judas, who was about to betray Him, asked in a low voice. "Is it I, Master?" And Jesus replied that it was indeed he who was to betray Him.

Jack: But, Grandma, why did not the other disciples take hold of Judas and lock him up to prevent him from betraying their Lord?

Grandma: In the first place, as our Lord and Judas spoke these few words in a low tone of voice, the other disciples probably did not hear. Moreover, they did not know of what betrayal the Lord spoke. If they had understood that He spoke of His betrayal unto death, they would have found it impossible to believe that one of their number could be guilty of such a crime.

CHAPTER XCIII.

CHRIST WASHES THE FEET OF HIS DISCIPLES.

Grandma: Jesus knew that the hour had come when he should suffer and die for men; and longing to prove His boundless love for us, He instituted the Blessed Sacrament of the Eucharist.

Louis: How did our Lord institute this Sacrament?

Grandma: By changing the bread and wine into His body and Blood, and giving it to his disciples to eat and drink, as your catechism teaches. And He gave to His disciples the power to do as He had done, and to continue this miracle, so that when He would have returned to His Father in Heaven, His disciples could unite themselves to Him in Holy Communion.

This blessed privilege is ours also, when we receive the Blessed Sacrament, for Christ loves us as He did His beloved Apostles. Before instituting the Holy Eucharist, our Lord washed the feet of His disciples.

Valentine: What! Our Lord washed the feet of His disciples—and why?

Grandma: To give them a lesson in humility, and to teach us the purity necessary to receive worthily the Body and Blood of our Lord in Holy Communion. We attain this purity of soul by repentance and a sincere confession on our part. This, added to the absolution of the priest, forgives our sins and cleanses the soul from all stains which mar its purity.

As I was about to tell you, before He instituted this great Sacrament our Lord rose from the table, took a basin which He filled with water, and having girded Himself with a towel, He washed the feet of His disciples and dried them with this cloth.

When our Lord knelt before Peter to wash his feet, Peter cried out: "Lord, dost Thou wash my feet? Jesus answered: What I do thou knowest not now; but thou shalt know hereafter. Peter saith to Him: Thou shalt never wash my feet. Jesus answered him: If I wash thee not, thou shalt have no part with Me. Then Peter saith to Him: Lord, not only my feet, but also my hands and my head. Jesus answered: He that is washed, needeth not but to wash his feet, but is clean wholly. And ye are clean, but not all."

Henrietta: Why does our Lord insist on washing Peter's feet when he doesn't wish it?

Grandma: Because, as I told you, our Lord was giving His disciples a lesson in humility, which was to be a lesson to Peter as well as to the other disciples. Moreover, our Lord here teaches that priests and bishops, and even the Holy Father, must humble

themselves and confess their sins as do all the faithful, that they may be forgiven.

Valentine: Why does our Lord say they are not
all pure?

Grandma: Because Jesus knew that Judas, who
was about to betray Him, was far from being clean
of heart.

CHAPTER XCIV.

THE INSTITUTION OF THE BLESSED EUCHARIST.

Grandma: After the washing of the feet, Christ sat down at table with His disciples and said to them: "Know you what I have done to you? You call Me Master and Lord; and you say well, for so I am. If then I, being your Lord and Master, have washed your feet, you ought also to wash one another's feet. For I have given you an example, that as I have done to you, so do you also."

The paschal lamb had been eaten, as ordained by the law, and the meal was drawing to a close; Jesus took the unleavened bread in His hands, blessed it, broke it, and gave it to His disciples, saying: "Take ye and eat. This is My Body. And having taken the chalice, giving thanks, He gave it to them, saying. Drink ye all of this. This is My Blood of the New Testament, which shall be shed for many unto remission of sins. Do this for a commemoration of Me."

Little Louis: Why does our Lord say: "This is My Body, this is My Blood," when He gave the Apostles only bread and wine?

Grandma: When Jesus pronounced these divine words: "This is My Body, this is My Blood," the bread and wine which He held in His hands were miraculously changed into His Body and Blood. This is called the Sacrament of the Holy Eucharist. It is a mystery of faith we cannot understand. Therefore, when Christ offered to His Apostles the unleavened bread and the chalice, only the appearances of bread and wine remained, and He said truly: "Take and eat, this is My Body; drink ye, this is My Blood."

In this great Sacrament our Lord proves His boundless love for us, by enabling us to unite ourselves to Him in Holy Communion whenever we will. For Jesus Christ gave to the Apostles and the priests, who are their successors, the power to continue this wonderful miracle.

Louis: Grandma, I have never received this Sacrament.

Grandma: You are too young yet. Soon you will make your first Communion, and receive for the first time the Body and Blood of our Lord. Before receiving this great favor, you must prepare with great care, learn your catechism, and try to understand how precious is this gift bestowed upon us by our Lord at the Last Supper.

Again Jesus spoke of His betrayal which was now near at hand, saying: "Woe to that man by whom the Son of Man shall be betrayed."

And John, the beloved disciple, was leaning on the bosom of Jesus.

Mary Theresa: How was he leaning on our Lord?

Grandma: As I have already explained, the Jews sat at table, and John was seated next to our Lord.

John, therefore, rested his head on the bosom of Jesus, and Peter made him a sign to ask the Master of whom He spoke: "Lord who is it?" whispered John. "He to whom I shall reach bread dipped." And, having moistened a piece of bread, He handed it to Judas Iscariot. As soon as Judas had eaten this piece of bread he rose from the table to carry out his purpose and betray the Master. "That which thou dost, do quickly," Jesus said to him.

But none of the disciples understood these words of Christ. They thought that Judas, having in charge the expenditures had something to buy for the festival.

When Judas had gone out, Jesus, together with His disciples, offered a prayer of thanksgiving.

Jane: For what did they say a prayer of thanksgiving?

Grandma: The disciples had just received their First Communion; and it was but just that they should return thanks to the good God for this favor granted to them, and to all men till the end of time, by the institution of the Holy Eucharist.

John, the disciple whom Jesus loved, wrote in his

Gospel a large portion of the beautiful words of our Lord on this occasion. I shall not repeat this discourse at the Last Supper, which, when you are older, you may read in the Gospel of St. John.

When Jesus had finished His discourse, and the hymn had been sung, He left the supper-room, followed by the eleven disciples, for the Mount of Olives, a hill outside of Jerusalem. Here was a garden known as Gethsemani where strangers coming to Jerusalem, rested before entering the city gates.

Jesus often withdrew to this secluded spot to spend the night in prayer. Judas had frequently accompanied Him, and hither he now led the soldiers of Caiphas, knowing they would here find the Christ absorbed in prayer.

BOOK SIXTH

The Passion and The Resurrection of Jesus

CHAPTER XCV.

THE AGONY IN THE GARDEN.

Grandma: It was late in the evening when they reached the Garden of Gethsemani and Jesus said to His disciples: "Sit you here, while I go yonder and pray." And he added: "Pray, lest ye enter into temptation."

Louis: What temptation does our Lord mean?

Grandma: The Passion of Christ was at hand. Our Lord knew this would be a trial to the Apostles, a temptation to their faith.

They were to see their Master, Whose divine power they had witnessed, seized, bound, mocked, scourged, and finally crucified by His enemies. This was, without doubt, a great trial to their belief in the divinity of Christ.

Jane: But Jesus had told them He was the Son of God.

Henrietta: And they had seen Him raise the dead Lazarus to life.

Elizabeth: And they had just been made strong by Holy Communion.

Grandma: All this is true, and they should have remained firm in their faith who had been privileged

to bear Him company for several years.   But, remember, they who had seen this same Christ, but a
short while before, powerful over life and death, were
about to see Him, who had proclaimed Himself
the Son of God, apparently powerless before His
enemies; yielding to suffering and dying as all men
die.

This was to be a severe test of their faith in His
word, and against this temptation our Lord bid them
pray.

And taking with Him Peter and James and John,
Jesus went further to a remote part of the garden,
and His Passion began.

Louis: What means the Passion?

Grandma: By Passion is meant the terrible
sufferings our Lord endured for us.   Of His own free
will, Christ yielded to suffering and to death, that
He might atone to His Father for the sins of men.

"My soul is sorrowful even unto death," He said
to His disciples; "stay you here, and watch with Me."

And overcome with sadness, He went a little
further from them to a corner of the Garden which
is still pointed out.   There He fell upon His face in
great agony.   All the sins of men, all the horror of
evil filled his soul and overpowered Him.   He who
loved His Father from all eternity, saw that He was
condemned to appear before Him bearing the sins
of the whole world, that He might expiate for the
wickedness and ingratitude of men.

Moreover, Christ saw in spirit how many of the human race would remain in their sins, in spite of the love He bore them, in spite even of the sufferings He bore *for* them. In agony of mind He cried out to His Father, if it were possible to let this suffering pass from Him. Nevertheless, He added: "Not My will but Thine be done."

So great was the agony of our Savior that his body was bathed in a bloody sweat while he prayed for the salvation of men.

Little Louis: How the Lord Jesus must have suffered, Grandma!

Grandma: Yes; He suffered more than any other creature ever has or ever will suffer. By this agony, this bloody sweat, these tears and supplications, our Lord and Savior Jesus Christ redeemed us, atoned for our sins. In other words, He, our Redeemer, suffered the punishment due to the human race, that we might be free to enter the kingdom of Heaven.

After this anguish of soul and body Jesus rose, unrefreshed and sad. Drawing near to His three disciples, He found them asleep, and very sadly He said to them: "What, could you not watch one hour with Me? Watch ye and pray that ye enter not into temptation."

Again He left them, and casting Himself on the ground, He repeated the same prayer: "O My

Father, if this chalice cannot pass except I drink it, Thy will be done."

This prayer, which should be our model in all our sufferings, our Savior repeated again and again in the agony in the Garden.

A second time He returned to His disciples, to find them again overcome with sleep, and, full of sadness that His disciples, even the beloved John, should thus leave Him alone in His agony, He resumed His prayer of submission and of supplication.

An Angel was sent from Heaven to comfort Him in His agony, and give Him strength to bear yet greater suffering. Our Savior here gives us a lesson on the necessity of prayer. The disciples, who neglected His warning and slept when they should have prayed for strength, failed when temptation came, and fled from danger, leaving their Master to suffer alone, as you will shortly see.

CHAPTER XCVI.

JUDAS BETRAYS CHRIST

Grandma: It was midnight, the traitor, Judas, was drawing near. Calm and serene, Jesus rose from prayer and approaching His disciples woke them, saying: "Rise; behold, he that will betray Me is at hand."

The disciples rose, frightened, for at that moment they heard the advancing tread of soldiers, accompanied by a large crowd carrying swords and staves.

Judas had given them a sign by which they should recognize Jesus: "Whomsoever I shall kiss that is He; hold Him fast."

Jack: How wicked Judas was. He deserved to be severely punished.

Grandma: He was terribly punished, as you will hear later.

And now, going up to Jesus, he said: "Hail, Master: and he kissed Him. Jesus said to him: Friend, whereto art thou come? Judas, dost thou betray the Son of Man with a kiss?"

Then Jesus stepped forward, toward the soldiers who had come to take Him prisoner, saying: "Whom seek ye?"

"Jesus of Nazareth," they cried out.

"I am He," answered the Savior. Hearing these words, the soldiers fell backwards on the ground overcome with terror.

Paul: I am glad of that. I hope they were killed!

Grandma: No; our Savior permitted them to rise unhurt. He was merciful and kind to the end. He gave these unfortunate creatures, for whom He was about to suffer and to die, the time to repent of their sins. Christ could have had legions of angels at His command, but here, for the last time, He showed His executioners that He had given Himself into their hands of His own free will.

Once more He told them He was Jesus of Nazareth, whom they sought, and they rose and bound Him roughly and led Him out of the Garden to the court of the High Priest, Annas.

The Apostles, who had failed to pray for strength, fled like cowards. Peter for a moment defended His Master, and drawing his sword, cut off the ear of one of the soldiers called Malchus.

Christ touched the wound and healed him, and He said to Peter: "Put up thy sword into its place. The chalice which my Father hath given Me, shall I not drink it?"

Jane: Of what chalice does our Lord speak?

Grandma: Our Lord spoke of the chalice of His Passion and Death. When we speak of drinking the chalice, we mean we accept with patience and resignation the sufferings and humiliations which are sent to us by the good God.

St. Peter fled with the other disciples, but from afar he and St. John followed the Master to the vestibule of the palace of Caiphas, where dwelt Annas, the High Priest. Unnoticed, they mingled in the crowd of Roman soldiers who were warming themselves at the fire built in the open court.

CHAPTER XCVII.

JESUS BEFORE ANNAS.

Grandma: Jesus was led before the High Priest Annas, who questioned Him on His doctrine and on His disciples.

Little Louis: What is doctrine?

Grandma: Doctrine is the teaching of our Lord and His Church on matters of faith. Jesus answered with gentle dignity: "I have spoken openly to the world; I have always taught in the synagogue and in the temple; why askest thou Me? Ask them who have heard what I have spoken; behold, they know what things I have said."

A rough soldier, deeming this dignified reply insulting to Annas, gave Jesus a blow in the face, saying: "Answerest Thou the High Priest so?"

Jesus replied: "If I have spoken ill give testimony of the evil; but if well, why strikest thou Me?"

Camille: How patient our Lord was!

Grandma: Yes; throughout His whole Passion our Savior gives us a wonderful lesson in humility, charity, and patience. And if soldiers are allowed to buffet Him, insult Him, and strike Him—it is only that we may learn to be strong against humiliation and injustice.

When our Lord and Savior suffered blows, insults, weariness, hunger, and thirst for love of us, how shall we dare complain of being severely or unjustly treated?

What He, the innocent Jesus, did for love of you, dear children, do you for love of Him. If a friend is false to you, think of Judas; if one strikes you, think of the blows Jesus received from these rough soldiers; and, in imitation of our Savior, keep your peace of soul and that deep humility full of gentleness which forgives all injuries.

CHAPTER XCVIII.

JESUS BEFORE CAIPHAS.

Grandma: Our Savior remained only a short while before the judgment seat of Annas. Caiphas had assembled the council of priests and princes, and they notified Annas to send them the prisoner. Jesus was, therefore, led before this council to be judged. These men were not seeking the truth, but an excuse to condemn the Christ, and therefore they bribed false witnesses to appear before this assembly and testify against Him.

These witnesses contradicted one another in their false testimony, and the high priest, angered at the silence of our Savior, asked Him sharply: "What, answerest Thou nothing to the things that these witness against Thee?"

But our Lord was silent. "And the high priest said to Him: I adjure Thee by the living God, that Thou tell us if Thou be the Christ, the Son of God."

Christ had not yet spoken before this gathering, but when Caiphas questioned Him in the name of God, He answered: "Thou hast said it. Nevertheless I say to you, hereafter you shall see the Son of Man sitting on the right hand of the power of God, and coming in the clouds of heaven."

Then the high priest rent his garments saying: "He hath blasphemed."

Louis: Why did Caiphas tear his garments?

Grandma: This was to the Jews a sign of great indignation, which the high priest thus hypocritically expressed.

"He is guilty of death," they all cried out at once. And, throwing themselves on Jesus, they spat on Him and struck Him in the face. The divine face of Christ was bruised and disfigured, and at every blow they mockingly asked: "Christ, prophesy who struck Thee."

Thus for several hours they made sport of Jesus and insulted Him. Then, still ill-treating Him, they dragged Him to one of the prisons of the palace.

CHAPTER XCIX.

PETER DENIES CHRIST.

Grandma: While the trial was going on before
Caiphas, Peter had remained in the courtyard with
the crowd. A few hours before he had assured our
Lord of his devotion to Him and to His cause.

He had protested his love to Christ in all sincerity,
though with some presumption in his own strength:
"Though all men shall be scandalized in Thee, I will
never be scandalized." To which our Lord had
answered sadly: "Amen I say to thee to-day, even
in this night, before the cock crow, thou wilt deny
Me thrice."

In spite of his Master's warning, Peter had slept
when he should have prayed for strength, and,
therefore, when temptation came he denied Christ
the Son of God.

A servant had noticed him as he entered the
courtyard and she asked him if he were not one of the
disciples of Jesus of Nazareth. Peter replied that
he knew Him not.

But troubled at the question and his untruthful
answer, he advanced to the group of soldiers to
warm himself by the open fire. A few moments

after another woman looked at him and pointed him out to those who stood near. Questioned a second time Peter again, and this time with an oath, denied that he knew the Christ.

An hour later one of the servants of Caiphas who had accompanied Judas to the Garden, entered the courtyard, recognized Peter, and said to him: "Did I not see thee in the garden with Him?" And Peter said: "Man, I know not what thou sayest."

"And immediately, while he was yet speaking, the cock crew."

At that moment Jesus passed by on His way to the prison of the Temple. Passing near Peter, He gave him a look full of reproach and compassion. Peter, overcome with sadness and sorrow at this glance from his Master, left the courtyard, and going out wept bitterly in repentance of his sin and of his unfaithfulness to the Master whom he loved.

CHAPTER C.

DESPAIR AND DEATH OF JUDAS.

Grandma: Peter wept in repentance of his sin. Though it was great, he did not despair of God's mercy. Judas also repented, as the Gospel tells us, but his sorrow was not a good repentance.

Elizabeth: How can that be, Grandma? It seems to me all repentance must be good.

Grandma: Repentance is good, and obtains God's forgiveness, when it comes from sorrow for having done evil and having offended the good God whom we love. The repentance of Judas sprang from sorrow for his great sin in betraying the Son of God, but, instead of praying God's forgiveness and weeping for his sins, as St. Peter had done, he despaired of God's mercy to forgive so great a crime. Judas foresaw a life of shame and dishonor in the eyes of all men as a traitor and an accomplice in the death of his Master, and this sense of shame overpowered all else, and led him to despair.

When he heard the condemnation of Jesus, he went to the princes and ancients of the people, to whom he had sold the Christ, and throwing down before them the thirty pieces of silver, he cried out:

"I have sinned in betraying innocent blood." The priests and princes only mocked him, and rushing out of the city, his heart full of rage and despair at the thought of his crime, "he hanged himself with a halter."

Our Lord had said: "Woe to that man by whom the Son of Man shall be betrayed. It were better for him, if that man had not been born."

Judas, by his despair, forfeited the grace of repentance. He should have called to mind the many instances he had witnessed of the mercy and goodness of the Savior for all sinners. He should have bewailed his crime and implored forgiveness, knowing that Christ would forgive his sin, however great.

Whatever sins we may commit, how great soever be our guilt, we must *never* despair of the mercy of God, which is as great as His love.

CHAPTER CI.

CHRIST BEFORE PILATE.

Grandma: At dawn of day Caiphas again assembled the Council and the Scribes and Pharisees. Jesus was brought before them a second time and questioned as on the day before. He testified again that He was Christ, the Son of God, made Man. He was condemned to die, but, as the Roman Governor alone could order the execution of a prisoner, Jesus was led to the palace of Pontius Pilate, who governed Jerusalem in the name of the Emperor of Rome.

Pilate was a weak and selfish character. He tried to please everybody, without regard to the justice of his judgments.

It was about six o'clock in the morning when Jesus was led before this tribunal. The Jews accused Him of many crimes and they testified that He had said He was the King of the Jews.

Pilate questioned Jesus, and was struck with His dignity and gentleness.

"Art Thou the King of the Jews?" he asked. And Jesus answered: "Thou hast said it. My kingdom is not of this world. If My kindgom were of this world, My servants would strive that I should not be delivered to the Jews. I came into the world that I should give testimony to the truth."

"And what is truth?" asked Pilate; but he did not wait for the reply of our Lord, for he did not care to know the truth. Turning to the Jews, he told them that he could find no fault to condemn in this Man, but that he would send Him to Herod, the Tetrarch of Galilee.

Paul: What is a Tetrarch?

Grandma: A Tetrarch is a king over a small province. Herod ruled over the province of Galilee. And Pilate, having learnt that Jesus was a Galilean, and desiring to make friends with Herod, sent him this prisoner from his own province.

CHAPTER CII.

CHRIST BEFORE HEROD.

Grandma: Herod, ruler of Galilee, was a cruel and arrogant prince. He had heard of Christ and of His miracles, and he hoped to see a display of His wonderful power. But the Son of God was silent in the presence of Herod. Angry and disappointed, Herod mocked Him, and, in derision, had Him clothed in a white garment, which in Galilee was the attire used to designate fools. Still mocking Jesus, he placed in His hand a reed as a mock scepter of royalty, and sent Him back to Pilate, accompanied by a derisive crowd, which, on His sorrowful way, struck and insulted the Divine Prisoner.

CHAPTER CIII.

CHRIST SENT BACK TO PILATE.

Grandma: Amid the cries of the populace, excited by the Pharisees, Christ appeared before Pilate's tribunal. Again he questioned Jesus, who remained silent, answering not a word to His accusers.

Jack: Why did He not answer? It seems to me He might have shown Pilate that He was innocent.

Grandma: Our Lord read the hearts of men, and He knew well that fear of the Emperor and of the Jewish people would prevent Pilate, who was weak, from being just. Moreover, when Pilate had asked Christ, "What is truth?" he had not waited for the Savior's answer. Now, Pilate was greatly perplexed at our Lord's silence. He did not wish to condemn Christ, whom he believed to be innocent, yet he wished to please this Jewish mob, for he feared to make enemies and thereby lose his position as Governor of Judea.

Too weak and cowardly to release the innocent prisoner who stood before him, Pilate thought of a plan whereby he might save Jesus from death, and yet not lose the favor of the people.

On the Feast of the Passover it was customary for the Emperor to forgive one prisoner sentenced to death. Barabbas, a robber, condemned to die, was waiting execution in the prisons of Jerusalem. Pilate had determined to release this man. However, knowing Barabbas was greatly feared for his many crimes, Pilate decided to offer to the crowd the release of the innocent Jesus in place of that of the wicked Barabbas.

But the crowd, whom the Pharisees had stirred into hatred of Jesus, called loudly to Pilate to forgive Barabbas, but not the Christ.

And Pilate asked: "What shall I do, then, with Jesus that is called Christ?"

"Crucify Him," answered this ungrateful people.

Thus Jesus saved Barabbas who deserved to die, as by His death on the cross He saved all the children of Adam from eternal death.

CHAPTER CIV.

CHRIST IS SCOURGED.

Grandma: Pilate still hesitated to give sentence of death: "I find no cause of death in Him," he repeated again to this angry crowd; but they only replied the louder: "Crucify Him! Crucify Him!"

Thinking to satisfy their rage, and save Jesus from death, he ordered Him to be scourged: I will chastise Him, therefore, and let Him go," he said, frightened at the clamor of the people.

Our Lord was given up to the executioners, who dragged Him to the courtyard of the palace. There the Roman soldiers stripped Him of the white robe in which Herod had clothed Him and, binding Him to a pillar, scourged Him with untold cruelty. His sacred flesh was torn by the heavy leather thongs used by the Romans in execution of this sentence of punishment.

Finally, wearied of striking, they unbound Jesus and, throwng over Him a scarlet cloak, they crowned Him with a crown of thorns whose sharp points pierced His brow; in His hands they placed the reed sceptre which Herod had forced on Him. "Hail, King of the Jews!" they mockingly said as they bent their knees before Him in mock adoration, and spat upon Him, struck Him, and reviled Him.

All this, my children, our Savior suffered for our sins, that he might redeem us and save us from the power of the evil one.

How ungrateful we are to forget the Passion of Christ and continue to offend Him, preferring our pleasure to the love He offers us. Man's ingratitude was one of our Lord's keenest sufferings, for He loves us and longs to save us; but against our own will He cannot do so.

All these cruel sufferings of Christ we make useless for us when we sin. Let us pray for one another, my children, that our hearts may overflow with love and gratitude towards this bountiful Savior, that we may profit by His sufferings and death, which purchased for us eternal life.

CHAPTER CV.

PILATE CONDEMNS CHRIST TO DEATH.

Grandma: Broken with suffering, crowned with thorns, the red robe hanging on His blood-covered shoulders, Christ was dragged before the judgment seat. Moved with pity at this spectacle, Pilate led Jesus out of the Hall of the Pretorium, in sight of all the people. He hoped the sight of their victim, disfigured and covered with blood, would inspire in their hearts some compassion.

"Behold the Man!" said Pilate. Yes, behold the Man whom they had tortured, treated with ignominy and despised.

"Behold the Man!" God Himself made man, suffering for those who will not recognize His Divinity. Behold the God-Man, whose life we have followed from Bethlehem to this day, who now of His own free will suffers and is about to die for all men whom He calls His brothers.

But the Jews showed no pity, their hearts were shut even at sight of so much agony. They wanted the ignominious death of the cross for this innocent victim. "Crucify Him! Crucify Him!" they cried, their voices growing louder and louder.

Pilate, stirred by so much ingratitude, spoke again:

"Why what evil hath this man done? I find no cause in Him. Shall I crucify your King?"

"We have no king but Caesar," cried the mob. "We have a law, and according to that law He ought to die, because He made Himself the Son of God; and if thou release this man thou art not Caesar's friend."

Hearing these words Pilate was filled with fear, and strove to smother the voice of his conscience. Ascending the steps of the tribunal which, according to the custom of ancient times, was in the open air, he called for a basin of water, and washing his hands in presence of the crowd, he said: "I am innocent of the blood of this just man; look you to it!"

"His blood be upon us and upon our children," answered the people. This people, until now the chosen people of God, blessed from the beginning with His special protection, now became accursed and, like Cain, wanderers on the surface of the earth; hated and despised by all men, as the executioners of Christ.

Having purified his hands, by which means he sought in vain to purify his soul, Pilate condemned Jesus to the most cruel and ignominious death, the death of the cross.

He ordered that the inscription which it was the custom to place on the cross over the head of the condemned man should be written in the three languages known as the sacred languages—Latin, Greek, and Hebrew: "Jesus of Nazareth, king of the Jews."

Louis: Why do you call them sacred languages, Grandma?

Grandma: Because the Psalms, the Old Testament, and the Gospels, and all those writings we call the Sacred Scriptures, are written in these languages.

This inscription did not please the Pharisees. They wanted it to read that Jesus had called Himself King of the Jews, not that He was their King.

Pilate despised the Jews and answered angrily: "What is written is written." He realized they had led him to commit a contemptible and cowardly deed, for which his conscience reproached him keenly.

It was about eight in the morning when Pilate pronounced the sentence condemning our Lord to the death of the cross.

To render the crucifixion more ignominious and more striking, two thieves who lay waiting execution in one of the prisons of the city were condemned to be crucified with Christ.

While all these preparations were taking place, the soldiers of Pilate continued to ill-treat the Savior as they had done before his condemnation.

When all was in readiness, Christ left the Pretorium for Golgotha, or Mount Calvary, carrying His own cross.

CHAPTER CVI.

CHRIST CARRIES HIS CROSS.

Grandma: The road which our Savior walked, between Pilate's palace and Mount Calvary, is still pointed out in Jerusalem and trod by many pilgrims, who thus really follow the foot-steps of Christ on His sorrowful journey. This we do also in spirit when we make the "Way of the Cross, or the Stations."

In spite of His great weakness Jesus was forced to carry His cross to Calvary, the place of His execution. Several times He fell beneath its heavy weight, which, none the less, was to Him a dear burden, since through its means He was to save the world.

If you go to Jerusalem you will see the spot where Jesus met His beloved mother accompanied by St. John, Mary Magdalene, and the other holy women. Here His mother waited to join Him in His sorrowful journey and be with Him to the end.

Tradition tells us that one of these holy women, filled with pity and compassion at sight of Jesus covered with sweat and blood, wiped His face with a napkin. Our Savior rewarded this act of courage and of love by leaving on this napkin the imprint of His divine face.

Jesus, and the thieves who were to be crucified with Him, finally reached Golgotha, the height of Mount Calvary, at about nine in the morning, or, as the Jews express it, at the third hour.

Elizabeth: Why do they call it the third hour?

Grandma: The Jews did not count the hours as we do. They counted from the rising of the sun to its setting. As all this happened in April when the sun rises at six o'clock, the third hour from its rising would be about nine o'clock. In like manner, the Gospel says Jesus died at the ninth hour, or three o'clock according to our manner of expressing it.

CHAPTER CVII.

CHRIST IS CRUCIFIED.

Grandma: Having reached the summit of Mount Calvary the executioners stripped our Lord of His robe and the mantle which covered His blood-stained shoulders. They laid the cross on the ground and upon it they stretched our Savior, nailing His feet and His outstretched hands to the wood of the cross. Above His thorn- rowned head they placed Pilate's inscription: "Jesus of Nazareth, King of the Jews!"

Then, lifting the cross, they stood it in the ground, in a hole dug for the purpose, and the Savior of the world was raised up, His arms outstretched, as if to embrace all men whom He had come to save.

On either side of our Savior they crucified the two thieves. The soldiers divided His garments among them; but as His robe was without seams and they would not cut it in two, they cast lots to determine who should have it.

All these details of the Passion of Christ had been predicted by the Prophets many centuries before the coming of the Messias.

Mount Calvary was crowded with people and the Pharisees were rejoicing over their triumph.

Sneeringly they spoke to Christ: "If Thou be the Son of God, come down from the Cross!" And others mockingly said: "He saved others, Himself He cannot save. If He be the King of Israel let Him come down from the cross and we will believe in Him."

Elizabeth: Why did not our Lord perform this miracle, and come down from the cross? They would have all been converted.

Grandma: This miracle would not have converted them any more than the raising of Lazarus, or the curing of the man born blind.

Remember the Pharisees were not ignorant, but their hearts were blinded by pride and hatred. Moreover, remember that at the very beginning of His Passion, our Lord had yielded to His Father all His divine power as the Son of God. For Himself He kept only the weakness of human nature as Son of Man.

The hour for miracles which would show His divine power was over. Yet, had the Jews but understood, the sacrifice of Christ on Mount Calvary was the greatest of all His miracles, a miracle of love.

CHAPTER CVIII.

THE CONVERSION OF THE GOOD THIEF.

Grandma: Above the tumult of the multitude; above their sneers and jeers, the voice of Christ was heard speaking to His Father, "Father, forgive them, for they know not what they do."

Madeleine: But it was their fault, Grandma, for our Lord had told them over and over who he was.

Grandma: Yes, surely He had, but once more He strives to touch their hearts; once more He appeals to His Father for their forgiveness. He does for them what he does for us, and we treat Him as did the Jews.

Elizabeth: Oh, Grandma! none of us ever treated our Lord as those dreadful people did.

Grandma: Each time we sin we strike our Lord, we insult Him. Each sin we commit was atoned for by the wounds in His hands and in His feet, by the precious blood He poured forth for us; by His agony and death. When we sin mortally we aid His executioners and crucify our Lord.

Madeleine: This is a fearful thought, Grandma, to think we are no better than those wicked men.

Grandma: We are as wicked as they when we commit mortal sins, which kill the grace of God in our souls. Being but weak creatures, we often fall into sins without reflection, yet without bad will. These are venial sins, as your catechism teaches, and these sins do not make us guilty of the death of Christ. However, we all, more or less, have been the cause of the suffering of Christ, which He willingly bore for us all. Therefore, we have good cause to weep over the passion of our Savior, and at the remembrance of our sins for which He atoned by His cruel sufferings and death.

At these wonderful words, full of mercy and love, "Father, forgive them, for they know not what they do," the heart of Dismas, the thief crucified at our Lord's right hand, was moved with deep and sincere contrition for his sins. At sight of so much love and mercy, he recognized the Son of God, and, turning towards Jesus, his eyes full of tears of sorrow, his soul full of deep humility and stirred by a great hope, he said: "Lord, remember me when Thou shalt come into Thy Kingdom. And Jesus said to him: Amen I say to thee, this day thou shalt be with Me in Paradise."

Jack: How happy the poor thief must have been!

Grandma: This blessed promise rejoiced the good thief in his last hour, and shows us it is never too late to repent. The greatest sinner may be forgiven if, with sincere contrition, he turns to God and begs His forgiveness.

But death often comes unawares and we must not trust for the grace of repentance on the last day, for we may not have time to turn to God, as did the good thief.

CHAPTER CIX.

CHRIST LEAVES HIS MOTHER TO ST. JOHN.

Grandma: For three hours our Savior hung upon the cross. From the sixth to the ninth hour, great darkness covered the earth.

Peter: Was it an eclipse of the sun such as I have studied about?

Grandma: No, this was a miraculous darkness which cannot be explained. We read of this fact in history as well as in the Gospels.

At the foot of the cross stood Mary the Mother of Jesus, calm and resigned, but her heart torn with sorrow.

Elizabeth: Poor Blessed Mother, it must have taken a great deal of courage to stand there.

Grandma: The Blessed Virgin had received, as Mother of God, a supernatural strength. The Gospel expressly says she "stood" at the foot of the cross, on which her beloved Son was nailed. She stood at the foot of the cross, like a priest at the alter offering up the sacrifice of the Mass. With her Son she accepted His sufferings in all submission to the will of the Father. With Him she offered up His life for the salvation of all men.

St. John was with the Blessed Virgin and also Mary Magdalene, and other good women, who had ministered to Jesus during His life and who loved Him dearly. Gathering His fast ebbing strength, Jesus looked lovingly and sadly at His Mother, and then at John His beloved disciple, and turning first to His mother, He said: "Woman, behold thy son!" And then to John: "Behold thy mother!"

All the human race was represented on Mt. Calvary, and He gave Mary to us all as our mother when He left her to St. John's care; and to His Mother He gave all mankind in the person of St. John.

Not content to leave us His body and His blood in the Blessed Eucharist to be our food and drink; here on Mount Calvary Jesus leaves us His own Mother, that she may protect and help us as a true mother would. And we must love and venerate the Mother of Jesus, now become our mother, and ask her for all our needs. She will hear us and obtain for us God's grace.

Thus our Lord Jesus and Mary are inseparable, for they are Mother and Son; and Mary shares the love of Christ Jesus for us all.

CHAPTER CX.

CHRIST DIES ON THE CROSS.

Grandma: The last solemn hour was drawing near. The darkness which covered the earth now began to disperse, disclosing to all the body of the Son of God hanging upon the cross. His blood had all been poured out, His strength was spent, His eyes were growing dim at the approach of death. That we might understand His anguish and the extreme loneliness of His last hour, Jesus cried out: "My God, My God, why hast Thou forsaken Me?" He no longer called God His Father He was bearing the sins of the whole world that He might expiate them; and in the sight of God He represented all sinners. He was now saddened, for His Father seemed to turn from Him, and He felt in His Humanity the estrangement from God's love which is due to sinners.

Again He spoke, His voice grown faint: "I thirst!"

A soldier standing by, moved with compassion, took a sponge dipped in vinegar and water, and placing it on the end of a reed, moistened the lips of the Savior.

This act of mercy had been announced by the Prophets, and Jesus, knowing that now all the prophecies had been fulfilled, and that the redemption of the world was accomplished, murmured: "It is consummated!" The purpose of His coming on this earth was completed.

And, lifting up His thorn crowned head, Jesus cried with a loud voice: "Father, into Thy hands I commend My spirit." And bowing His head, our Redeemer died.

CHAPTER CXI.

CHRIST IS BURIED.

After a few moments of silence, Grandma took up again the thread of the story: The Son of God had died; God, the creator of the earth and sea and sky, God, who commands life and death, had given up His life. The gates of heaven had been closed since the sin of the first man, Adam. This sin, which your catechism teaches is called original sin, was now atoned for. Henceforth man was saved and could enter heaven if he kept God's law.

Our Savior died on Good Friday. At his death the earth trembled, the rock of Mount Calvary was rent in two, and a great terror spread over Jerusalem. The curtain in the Temple, which separated the Holy of Holies from the Temple was torn from top to bottom. This showed that the Old Law was done away with; the New Law stood in its place.

At our Lord's death, His soul descended into Limbo. This was a place where the souls of the just who had died before the coming of Christ waited for the Redemption, that they might enter heaven. Here our Lord went to announce the joyful tidings that heaven was opened and sin atoned for and all mankind at peace with heaven.

Our Lord's body still hung on the cross. Night was drawing near, and as the next day was the Sabbath day, the bodies on Mount Calvary had to be buried without delay.

To make sure that the two thieves were dead, the soldiers broke their legs. When they came to Jesus they found He was dead, but to make sure that the body was lifeless, one of the soldiers pierced His side with a lance.

St. John, who still stood at the foot of the cross, tells us in the Gospel which he wrote, that from this wound flowed water and blood; which represents the two sacraments of Baptism and the Holy Eucharist.

One of the disciples, who was rich and powerful, named Joseph of Arimathea, went to Pilate and asked permission to take the body of our Lord and bury it in a sepulchre he owned at the foot of Mount Calvary.

Pilate, having made sure Christ was dead, granted the request.

Joseph, aided by St. John and other disciples, took the body of Christ down from the cross and gently laid it in the arms of His Mother. From His brow they lifted the cruel crown of thorns, and drew out the nails from His wounded hands and feet. They wrapped His body in a winding sheet and covered His head with a cloth. Then they gently carried their most precious burden to the tomb which Joseph of Arimathea had cut in the rock. This sepulchre of Christ is still shown and visited by pilgrims from all over the world. After one last look, one last kiss, Mary, now indeed the Mother of Sorrows, left Christ in the sepulchre and together with John, her adopted son, and the holy women, returned sadly to Jerusalem.

The priests and Pharisees had, from a distance, witnessed all these sad ceremonies. They remembered Jesus had said that He would rise on the third day after His death. They went, therefore, to Pilate, asking him for soldiers to guard the tomb "for fear" they said, "that His disciples should come and steal Him away and tell he people He is risen from the dead." Pilate, answered: "You have a guard, guard it as you know."

Then with great care the Jews shut the entrance to the sepulchre with a great stone sealed with the seal of the Temple, and around it set a guard of soldiers to watch day and night and prevent its being broken into.

Peter: They thought this would prevent Jesus from rising from the dead. No doubt when He rose in spite of them they were converted.

Grandma: This miracle, of which I shall tell you, did not convert them any more than all former miracles of our Lord had done, and this notwithstanding that all these precautions which they took to prevent this great miracle only helped to render the resurrection of Christ more striking.

CHAPTER CXII.

RESURRECTION OF CHRIST.

Grandma: On fourteen different occasions during His life, our Lord had foretold His resurrection after death. He had offered this miracle to the Apostles and to the Jews as a sign of His Divinity; as a sign that He was truly God, equal to His Father, ruler over life and death. The enemies of Christ so fully understood the great importance of the resurrection as a proof of Christ's Divine mission, that they took every means to prevent its possibility. By their care to prevent it they made the resurrection of Christ only the more remarkable.

The very soldiers who guarded the tomb of Christ witnessed His glorious resurrection. The disciples had spent the Sabbath day overpowered with grief. They had forgotten His promise that He would rise again on the third day. He whom they loved was dead and it was hard to believe in His divinity in this dark hour of sorrow. The holy women, on their return to Jerusalem, had bought one hundred pounds of sweet spices that they might, when the Sabbath day would be over, embalm the body of Jesus.

At dawn on Easter Sunday the Holy Sepulchre was broken open. An angel from heaven, brighter than the sun, appeared before the astonished guards and rolled back the stone which blocked the sepulchre. The guards fell back as if dead, so great was their fear; and as soon as they were able to rise they fled to the city. The Son of God had risen from the dead. He had fulfilled the prophecy which He had made. Our Lord had conquered death for us, all sons of Adam.

Jack: How can death be conquered. It is not a man you can meet and fight?

Grandma: Our Lord conquered death by His resurrection, that is to say that, by atoning for the sins of man, He gave to souls eternal life and to our bodies the power to rise again from the dead on the last day. Even as Christ took up His body again, so shall we all.

If we have been faithful here on this earth, where we are tried, our bodies will share in our reward in heaven, as they will share in our eternal punishment if we are unfaithful. Then the guards fled to the city and told the High Priests and princes what had happened, but they continued unbelieving. Still full of hatred and envy, they gave money to the soldiers as a bribe that they might say that during the night the disciples had stolen away the body of Jesus.

Jane: Did the people believe this wicked story?

Grandma: No; because the miracle was too evident. First the guards could not all have slept at once and so soundly that the noise of the breaking of the sepulchre could not have wakened them. Moreover, no one could readily believe that the disciples, who were so timid that they had fled from their Master at the first sign of danger, should have become strong and fearless enough to fight the armed men who were watching the sepulchre. Then, too, if the soldiers had slept while on duty the High Priests and princes would have thrown them into prison and used them as witnesses before the people against the disciples of Christ instead of bribing them to keep silence.

The news of the resurrection of our Lord soon spread far and wide; and prepared the way for the thousands of conversions brought about later on by the preaching of St. Peter and the other Apostles.

CHAPTER CXIII.

MARY MAGDALENE AT THE TOMB OF CHRIST.

Grandma: Very early in the morning of Easter Sunday Mary Magdalene set out to visit the Holy Sepulchre. Mary was the converted sinner who had bathed the feet of Christ with tears of repentance, and who had accompanied the Blessed Mother to Calvary and stood with her at the foot of the Cross. While she was wending her way to the sepulchre, thinking sadly of Christ lying in the tomb, He had already risen from the dead.

When Mary Magdalene reached the spot the guards fled, and she saw with amazement that the door was thrown open and the heavy stone rolled back. She cast a quick glance into the tomb and not finding the body of her Savior, ran back in all haste to the city to warn St. Peter and the other disciples.

Peter and John made haste and followed Mary to the sepulchre. St. John, who was much younger, outran Peter and was the first to reach the spot. They looked and found the sepulchre empty, as Mary had told them.

Peering into the dark tomb they saw the shroud lying there which the risen Christ had cast off, and the napkins which had wrapped His head folded apart.

The two disciples forgot at this moment the promise of the resurrection, and thinking the body of their Master had been stolen, they were filled with distress and alarm, and hastened to tell the other disciples what they had seen.

Notice all these details, my children, for they show plainly that the Apostles had had no thought, as the Jews suspected, of taking away the body of Christ to prove his resurrection. They did not even believe Christ would fulfill His promise and rise from the dead.

CHAPTER CXIV

CHRIST APPEARS TO MARY MAGDALENE.

Grandma   Mary Magdalene remained at the holy sepulchre, after Peter and John had gone back to tell the Apostles of the event they had witnessed.

Left alone, Mary knelt near the tomb, thinking of Him whom she loved, who had been laid there. Now she knew not even where His body lay.

Drawing nearer she peered into the open sepulchre and saw two Angels clothed in white seated on either side "where the body of Jesus had been laid."

They spoke to her: "Woman, why weepest thou?"

Weeping bitterly, Mary replied: "Because they have taken away my Lord; and I know not where they have laid Him."

While speaking she perceived near her a man whom she took to be the gardener who had charge of the grounds. Tears obscured her vison and she said to him: "Sir, if thou hast taken Him hence, tell me where thou hast laid Him."

A voice which she knew well, and loved beyond all other voices, called her by name: "Mary!"

She started up in glad surprise and saw her beloved Savior standing before her. In her joy she cast herself at His feet to cover them anew with kisses. But Jesus said to her: "Do not touch Me, for I am not yet ascended to My Father. But go to My brethren, and say to them: I ascend to My Father and to your Father, to My God and to your God."

Louis: Why does our Lord, who is God, say He is going to God?

Grandma: Because,.as you know, He was true man as well as true God. As man, Jesus prayed, adored God, and obeyed Him, even as we do. In His human nature, God was truly His God. Mary Magdalene hastened to obey her Master, and, her heart full of joy, she ran to announce to the disciples the glad tidings of the resurrection. But they did not believe Mary's testimony.

Elizabeth: It is surprising that the Apostles would not believe in the resurrection which Jesus had foretold and which Mary Magdalene had seen with her own eyes. Really these men did not deserve the love Jesus bore them.

Grandma: Remember the Apostles were still weak and ignorant men. They had not as yet received the Holy Ghost, who confirmed their faith and enlightened their understanding. You will see that after the coming of the Holy Spirit, these ignorant weak, and timid men became eloquent, full of courage and learning, and converted thousands of unbelievers to the Faith.

CHAPTER CXV.

CHRIST APPEARS TO THE HOLY WOMEN.

Grandma: A few hours later Mary, the mother of James and Solome, and two other holy women, went to the Holy Sepulchre to help Mary Magdalene, embalm the body of Jesus. On the way they asked each other anxiously how they would enter the sepulchre, thinking of the huge stone which closed its entrance. As they drew nearer, they saw with surprise the stone rolled back, the sepulchre opened and deserted.

They hastened forward and looked into the tomb, but in vain, the body of their Lord was not there. They were seized with consternation and fright as they saw a bright angel seated at the head of the Sepulchre; but the angel reassured them, saying: "Be not affrighted; you seek Jesus of Nazareth, who was crucified: He is risen, as He said, He is not here; behold the place where they laid Him. But go, tell His disciples and Peter that He goeth before you into Galilee; there you shall see Him, as He told you."

Henry: Why does the angel say they are to tell Peter especially?

Grandma: Our Lord had chosen St. Peter to be Head of the Apostles, and they recognized him as their chief; and the angel here confirms his headship.

At the words of the angel, they recalled the prophecy of our Lord and, filled with awe and wonder, they sped back to Jerusalem to bear the glad tidings to the disciples. But, behold, as they made haste, Christ Himself stood before them. "Hail!" he said.

They cast themselves at His feet and adored Him. Jesus spoke to them: "Fear not, go tell My brethren that they depart into Galilee and there they shall see Me." Saying this, Christ disappeared and the holy women did as He told them; but the Apostles believed their word no more than they had believed Mary Magdalene. They persisted in their incredulity.

Elizabeth: It seems to me the Apostles are very stubborn. I would have believed.

Grandma: God permitted their presistent incredulity to aid *our* faith. The more incredulous they were in the beginning, the greater the value of their word to us when they came to believe in the resurrection. The testimony they gave of the risen Christ, a testimony they confirmed with their blood, is all the stronger because of their slowness of belief.

CHAPTER CXVI.

CHRIST APPEARS TO THE DISCIPLES ON THE ROAD TO EMMAUS.

Grandma: Towards evening on the day of the resurrection, two of the disciples were walking on the road to Emmaus, a small village outside of Jerusalem. On the way they were conversing sadly together of the coming of the Messias, and of His crucifixion.

Jesus drew near, but they did not know Him; and walking on with them, He asked them the cause of their sadness. Willingly the disciples told Him of the events of the past few days, and they added sadly: "We indeed hoped He would have delivered Israel, and now, besides all this, this is the third day since these things were done; and some of the women of our company affrighted us, who before it was light were at the sepulchre, and not finding His body, came, saying that they had also seen a vision of angels who say that He is alive. And some of our people went to the sepulchre and found it so as the women had said, but Him they found not."

Then Jesus said to them: "O foolish and slow of heart to believe in all things which the prophets have spoken. Ought not Christ to have suffered these things, and so to enter into His glory?"

And then, beginning from Moses and the other prophets, He explained to them the prophecies and how they had all foretold the suffering and death of Christ and His glorious resurrection. Finally they reached Emmaus, and as their divine companion seemed about to leave them, eagerly the disciples begged Him to stay, saying entreating: "Stay with us, for it is late, and the day is drawing to a close."

Jesus consented, and they entered the traveler's inn to partake of the evening meal together. Seated at table, Jesus took the bread in His hands, blessed it, broke it, and gave it to His companions. In His blessed hands the bread was changed into His Sacred Body and these happy disciples received Communion from our Lord's hands. Then their eyes were opened and they knew their Master, who disappeared before them. They said to one another: "Were not our hearts all burning within us, while He talked with us on the way?" They knew at last that their companion was none other than the risen Savior, and they hastened back to Jerusalem to announce the glad tidings to the other disciples.

But even then the disciples would not believe that the crucified Jesus was now alive and risen from the dead.

CHAPTER CXVII.

CHRIST APPEARS TO THE DISCIPLES GATHERED TOGETHER.

Grandma: The disciples were assembled together and the doors shut. No doubt they were discussing among themselves the wonders they had heard. Suddenly Jesus stood before them, and spoke: "Peace be to you; it is I, fear not."

But they were frightened, for they thought they saw a ghost. But the sweet voice they knew so well added: "Why are you troubled, and why do thoughts arise in your hearts?" And showing them His hands and His feet, which bore the holes made by the nails, He added. "See My hands and My feet, it is I Myself; handle, and see: for a spirit hath not flesh and bones, as you see Me to have."

And while the disciples hesitated, divided between hope and fear, the Good Master, always patient, offered them one last sign to convince them: "Have you here anything to eat?" He asked. They offered Him a piece of broiled fish and some honey. He ate of these, not because He was hungry, but to prove to the disciples that He was truly risen from the dead. Then He distributed among them what was left.

At last the disciples were convinced. They saw with their own eyes, they touched with their own hands, their risen Lord. Downcast and disheartened but a moment before, now they were full of joy and gladness. They adored Christ Jesus, risen from the dead. Then our Lord reproached them for the hardness of their hearts and their slowness of belief, and He enlightened their hearts that they might understand that what the Prophets had foretold concerning Him had now been accomplished in His life, death, and glorious resurrection.

He said to them again: "Peace be to you. As the Father hath sent Me, I also send you. When He had said this, He breathed on them; and He said to them: Receive ye the Holy Ghost. Whose sins you shall forgive, they are forgiven them; and whose sins you shall retain, they are retained."

Thus Christ instituted the Sacrament of Penance, in which sacrament we confess our sins and obtain their forgiveness.

Henry: But our Lord don't say we have to confess our sins? He only speaks of forgiveness of sins.

Grandma: When our Lord gave to His Apostles and to their successors power to forgive and retain sins, He knew there would be sins in the lives of men which would need forgiveness. These sins must

be made known that they may be forgiven or retained. This is confession—the telling of our sins,
that we may receive absolution for them from one
who has the power to forgive them.

The priest has likewise the power to withhold
forgiveness if he finds the penitent has not repented
for his sins and has no firm purpose of amendment.

Remember, therefore, children, that the Sacrament of Penance was not instituted by man, but by
Christ Himself when He said to His Apostles:
"Whose sins you shall forgive, they are forgiven
them; and whose sins you shall retain, they are
retained."

CHAPTER CXVIII.

THE INCREDULITY OF THOMAS.

Grandma: When Christ had appeared to the Apostles gathered together, Thomas, one of the twelve, was not with them. When he joined the other disciples and they told him the glad news of how they had seen and talked with their Lord, and even eaten with Him, Thomas refused to believe, He only answered: "Except I shall see in His hands the print of the nails and put my finger into the place of the nails, and put my hand into His side, I will not believe."

Eight days later the Apostles were again gathered together and Thomas was with them. The doors and windows were closed as formerly. Suddenly Jesus stood in their midst and said to them:

"Peace be with you." And turning to Thomas He said: "Put in thy finger hither, and see My hands; and bring hither thy hand, and put it into My side; and be not faithless but believing."

The unbelieving Apostle, now convinced, fell at the feet of Christ, full of faith and sorrow, crying out: "My Lord and my God."

Jesus said to him reproachfully: "Because thou hast seen Me, Thomas, thou hast believed; blessed are they that have not seen, and have believed."

Jane: We believe without seeing, do we not, Grandma?

Grandma: Surely it is of us all our Lord here speaks: "Blessed are they who believe without seeing." But it is not sufficient for us to have faith; we must live according to our faith by practicing the virtues of which our Lord gave us the example throughout His life; and by living our lives according to His teachings.

CHAPTER CXIX.

ST. PETER APPOINTED HEAD OF THE CHURCH.

Grandma: After His glorious resurrection, Christ remained forty days on earth. He appeared frequently to the Apostles, now on the shores of the Lake of Galilee, now in the upper room where the Last Supper had been celebrated, and where they assembled to pray and talk together of the wonders they had witnessed.

During these forty days Christ taught the Apostles all things needful to the establishment of His Church. He gave them power to continue His work.

On one of these occasions, on the shores of the Lake of Galilee, Christ spoke to St. Peter, selecting him out from among his brethren: "Simon, son of John, lovest thou Me more than these?"

Peter answered humbly: "Yea, Lord, Thou knowest that I love Thee."

"Feed My lambs," our Lord replied.

A second time Jesus asked him the self-same question; "Simon, lovest thou Me?"

Again Peter answered eagerly: "Lord, Thou knowest that I love Thee."

And again our Lord said to him: "Feed My lambs."

Three times, as you know, Peter had denied Christ, and Christ now asked of him a third assurance of his love and devotion; again he questioned him: "Lovest thou Me?"

Very humbly, having in mind his past presumption and sin, Peter replied: "Lord, Thou knowest all things: Thou knowest that I love Thee."

Then Jesus looked on him lovingly and said: "Feed My sheep."

Paul: Of what lambs and of what sheep was our Lord speaking?

Grandma: The lambs of which our Lord spoke are all the faithful of the Church of Christ. The sheep are the pastors, the bishops, the priests, who baptize us and teach us all truths. Sheep and lambs all form one flock, under the guidance of one shepherd, St. Peter and his successors, our Holy Father the Pope, the Vicar of Christ on earth. Therefore, we all obey the Holy Father as Christ's representative, the successor of St. Peter, whom Christ Jesus appointed Head of His Church on earth.

CHAPTER CXX.

CHRIST ASCENDS INTO HEAVEN.

Grandma: The forty days following the resurrection were over. The time had come for Christ to leave this earth; His disciples and Apostles were gathered around Him for the last time. Jesus led this band of faithful ones to the brow of the Mount of Olives, outside of Jerusalem. He spoke to the Apostles saying: "Thus it is written, and thus it behooved Christ to suffer, and to rise again from the dead the third day. And you are witnesses of these things unto all nations, beginning at Jerusalem. And I send the promise of My Father upon you; but stay you in the city, till you be endued with power from on high."

And lifting up His hands He blessed them and said to them: "Go ye into the world, whole and preach the Gospel to every creature. Baptize them in the name of the Father, and of the Son, and of the Holy Ghost. Teaching them to observe all things whatsoever I have commanded you; and behold I am with you all days, even to the consummation of the world."

Thus solemnly our Lord took leave of His Apostles. And behold He was raised up before them and a bright cloud hid Him from their sight. Thus Christ "departed from them and was carried up to Heaven."

The mystery of the Redemption was accomplished, original sin atoned for, the Church of Christ established, and the Blessed Eucharist instituted. Through this Sacrament Jesus Christ remains with us, hidden under the appearances of bread and wine, though His visible bodily presence has been withdrawn from this earth.